CW00833135

*Inkpaduta*

# *Inkpaduta*

## Dakota Leader

PAUL N. BECK

University of Oklahoma Press : Norman

Also by Paul N. Beck

*Soldier, Settler, and Sioux: Fort Ridgely and the Minnesota River Valley, 1853–1867* (Sioux Falls, S.Dak, 2000)
*The First Sioux War: The Grattan Fight and Blue Water Creek, 1854–1856* (Lanham, Md., 2004)

Library of Congress Cataloging-in-Publication Data

Beck, Paul Norman, 1958–
   Inkpaduta : Dakota leader / Paul N. Beck.
      p. cm.
   Includes bibliographical references and index.
   ISBN 978-0-8061-3950-0 (hardcover : alk. paper) 1. Inkpaduta, d. ca.
1879. 2. Dakota Indians — Kings and rulers — Biography. 3. Dakota
Indians — Wars. 4. Dakota Indians — History — Sources. I. Title.
   E99.D1I357 2008
   978.004′9752 — dc22
   [B]                                                      2008005615

The paper in this book meets the guidelines for permanence and durability of the Committee on Production Guidelines for Book Longevity of the Council on Library Resources, Inc. ∞

1  2  3  4  5  6  7  8  9  10

To Ian and Lauren

# Contents

# *Illustrations*

## FIGURES

## MAPS

# *Preface*

I grew up on a farm near St. James, Minnesota, not far from the Watonwan River, believed to be the birthplace of Inkpaduta. Perhaps that sparked an early interest in this Dakota leader. Childhood visits to Spirit Lake, Iowa; Jackson (formerly Springfield), Minnesota; and Fort Ridgely led me to believe that Inkpaduta was a man of evil intentions whose passion was the murdering of white settlers. This view obviously came only from what whites had written about him.

Many years later, after completing my Ph.D. program, I started doing research on Inkpaduta for a possible book. At first assuming Inkpaduta was a historical villain, I quickly reversed my opinion. The more I read, the more I discovered that false information, legends, and white bias had created a mythical Inkpaduta who did not resemble the real man I was researching. My review of the attitudes of the Dakotas, from both Inkpaduta's time and the present day, revealed a totally different Inkpaduta: a great leader who refused to sell his tribal lands and fought to protect them; a loving father who cared for his wives and children; a man who at times could act recklessly but mostly lived at peace with whites and simply wanted to live according to the traditional ways of his people.

For these reasons I believed a book on Inkpaduta—the real Inkpaduta, not the "bogeyman" of white legends—was needed. Much of what has been written about Inkpaduta comes from whites who often feared and hated him. Moreover, after the Spirit Lake massacre in 1857, Inkpaduta was rarely seen by whites, thus making positive statements on his whereabouts and actions difficult. American Indian sources helped clarify certain events in his life. These sources also give a much needed balance in interpreting Inkpaduta's place in history.

Still, many aspects of Inkpaduta's life, including his journeys in the West after the Spirit Lake massacre, remain vague. Because of the lack of sources and documentation, Inkpaduta will likely always remain something of a mystery. It is my hope that this first scholarly look at Inkpaduta and the myths that surround his life will lead to further investigation into the life of this important Dakota leader.

# Acknowledgments

Many people have contributed their time, efforts, and encouragement in order to bring this book into being. To all of them, I say thank you and extend my true gratitude for their assistance. Any errors in the book are solely my own.

I would particularly like to thank the staffs of the Minnesota Historical Society, the State Historical Society of Iowa, the South Dakota Historical Society, the Wisconsin Lutheran College Library, and the Milwaukee Public Library. Without their aid and assistance, research for the book would have been impossible.

I am also deeply indebted to the University of Oklahoma Press. My appreciation to all the staff there who have been so helpful to me during this process. In particular, I would like to thank acquisitions editor Alessandra Jacobi Tamulevich for her guidance and professionalism and associate editor Jay Dew and copyeditor Robert Fullilove for their work on the manuscript.

A number of individuals deserve special recognition: Gary Clayton Anderson, Kingsley Bray, and Raymond Bucko all either read portions of the manuscript or reviewed it for possible publication; their suggestions to improve the book were greatly appreciated and helpful.

Ladonna Allard, Danny Seaboy, Ambrose Little Ghost, and Leonard Wabasha provided me with insights into how the Dakotas/Lakotas remember Inkpaduta; their information provided a much needed perspective to help balance the opinions about Inkpaduta. Gary Kraft did excellent work on the maps for the book.

Laura Abing and Brigid Rafferty assisted in editing the manuscript in its early stages; their expertise proved invaluable.

Diane Koser, faculty secretary at WLC, came through with technical assistance when I ran out of patience with my word processor and helped put the final manuscript together.

Dr. Jerry Poppe, colleague and friend, gave encouragement; his support kept the project moving forward.

My wife, Sheila, was always there when I needed her and took care of our two small children when I was away researching and writing. Saying thank you is simply not enough.

Finally, and always, Pro Gloria Dei.

# Introduction

The year 2007 marked the 150th anniversary of the Spirit Lake massacre. In March 1857 a small band of hungry, cold, and persecuted Wahpekute Dakotas led by Inkpaduta killed thirty-nine men, women, and children at Spirit Lake and in the small village of Springfield in the border region of Iowa and Minnesota. The victims had done nothing to provoke such an attack, but an extremely harsh winter, coupled with the actions of other settlers in Iowa, led Inkpaduta and his band to take out their revenge. A brutal massacre, the killings alarmed settlers throughout the Midwest, causing widespread panic and retaliatory attacks on bands of innocent Dakotas. The hysteria caused by Inkpaduta's attacks was even greater than the panicked reaction to the far more serious Dakota War of 1862. That the United States Army consistently failed to apprehend and punish Inkpaduta for the massacre only added to his infamy. Time and again, attempts to capture the elusive Inkpaduta ended in failure, often due to the support he received from other Dakotas, who saw him as a good man resisting the encroachment of whites.

Inkpaduta became a frontier "bogeyman," always lurking, plotting, and raiding everywhere from the Canadian border to Kansas. His hatred of whites was said to know no limits. Long before Little Crow, Sitting Bull, or Crazy Horse, Inkpaduta was the Dakota chief best known and most feared by whites.

When news of the Spirit Lake massacre broke across the Midwest, many settlers immediately considered Inkpaduta the quintessential savage. To them, Inkpaduta was a man who hated whites and wished to harm them, a man who lived for war and violence with no love or compassion in him. This image of Inkpaduta remains to the present day. In memory, if not in historical fact, Inkpaduta is a prime example of the savage Indian feared by whites. To make him conform to this image, writers dealing with Inkpaduta, the massacre, the history of the Dakotas, or the Midwest region have merged every attribute of evil into Inkpaduta's life. His real-life experiences were altered or fabricated to fit the demonized view of him held by whites.

Shortly after the massacre, information about Inkpaduta and his band began to appear. On May 20, 1857, the *St. Paul Courier*, claimed Inkpaduta and his people were renegades, "outcasts, execrated by their own people, whose blood they desire." Charles Flandrau, a former Indian agent, soon described Inkpaduta as one of the "best haters of the whites in the whole Sioux nation." This opinion was seconded by L. P. Lee, who wrote one of the first accounts of the Spirit Lake massacre. Lee reported that Inkpaduta was "universally reputed as one of the most blood-thirsty Indian leaders" and held a "deep hatred for the whites."[1] Within months of the massacre, whites were depicting Inkpaduta as a renegade despised by his own people and an intense hater of all whites.

By the start of the twentieth century, writers for the Iowa and Minnesota historical societies were busily collecting the histories of their states; consequently, new accusations were leveled against Inkpaduta: he was the bloodthirsty murderer not only of innocent white settlers but of his own people too. He was reported to have killed Tasagi, the leader of the Wahpekutes; Wamundiyakapi, Tasagi's son and heir; and his own father, Wamdisapa.

During this period, the man most responsible for promoting Inkpaduta as an unrelenting savage was Doane Robinson. Robinson had been a teacher, lawyer, and newspaper editor before becoming the state historian for South Dakota. Intending to write a book on Inkpaduta, Robinson set about collecting information on the Sioux leader, meeting with members of the Dakota nation but rarely citing his sources. Robinson was convinced of Inkpaduta's wickedness, comparing him to Satan and proclaiming, "He was a fiend incarnate, of whom there is not recorded one single act that was not steeped in blood-thirsty deviltry thrice refined." Inkpaduta was "cruel, vindictive, passionate and conscienceless" and did not possess a "single noble trait of character."[2] He was the embodiment of all the fears and stereotypes whites held of those Native Americans still living free on the frontier.

Robinson added more infamy to Inkpaduta's legend. He maintained that Inkpaduta's father, Wamdisapa, was also an evil renegade who had been thrown out of the Wahpekute band for refusing to stop fighting the Sac and Fox tribe. Wamdisapa presumably taught Inkpaduta his violent ways, but Robinson observed that the son became "more treacherous, blood-thirsty and adroit than his father." Robinson also alleged Inkpaduta was a key instigator in the Dakota War of 1862, maintaining: "His hands were among the bloodiest." After the Dakotas lost the war, Robinson wrote that Inkpaduta continued to lead the Sioux against the U.S. Army in the Dakota Territory before later participating in Red Cloud's War and the Fetterman Fight in Wyoming. According to Robinson, Inkpaduta was everywhere from the Canadian border to Kansas raiding and killing. He maintained, "Wherever an outrage was committed the tracks of the bloody-handed chief might have been found nearby."[3] Inkpaduta's image was one of a man constantly at war with whites, whom he hated, always plotting against them, arousing the Dakotas to fight, and personally behind every raid and violent act perpetrated against frontier settlers.

Robinson's condemnations of Inkpaduta, along with similar views expressed by other writers of the era, have influenced whites' perceptions of Inkpaduta to the present day. In his 1998 book, *The Dakota War: The United States Army versus the Sioux, 1862–1865*, Michael Clodfelter continued to demonize Inkpaduta. Basing his information heavily on Robinson's writings, Clodfelter damned Inkpaduta as "almost demented" and restated many of the old accusations. "From Spirit Lake to the last battles of the Badlands," argued Clodfelter, "Inkpaduta was present, in spirit if not always in body, instigating, inflaming."[4]

Finally, amateur historian Maxwell Van Nuys, in his self-published biography, *Inkpaduta — the Scarlet Point: Terror of the Dakota Frontier and Secret Hero of the Sioux*, championed the now almost universally accepted white memory of Inkpaduta but added a new twist. The Dakotas, especially the Lakotas, admired Inkpaduta for his hatred of whites and willingly followed his leadership in a series of frontier wars from 1862 to 1876. To Van Nuys, Inkpaduta was not just a renegade Wahpekute set on deviltry but an evil genius bent on making war on whites whenever he could rally the Sioux to support his efforts. Van Nuys goes so far as to name Inkpaduta the chief architect of Custer's defeat at the Little Big Horn.[5]

However popular this depiction of Inkpaduta remains, it leaves much to be desired from the historian's point of view. Most of the works dealing with Inkpaduta suffer from a lack of documentation. It is as if there were a contest among writers to see who could most blacken Inkpaduta's character. In fact, besides the

Spirit Lake massacre, little solid evidence exists for this demonizing of Inkpaduta. Rumors became legends and were written as
fact. Dakota testimonies of Inkpaduta, which portray him quite
differently, were allowed no credence and were rarely even mentioned in white accounts of Inkpaduta. The Dakotas hold Inkpaduta in great respect as a fierce warrior who fought to maintain
the lands and culture of his people. Inkpaduta was not only a
patriot, but a good husband and father who cared for his people.
Driven to oppose encroaching whites, Inkpaduta fought only to
survive and protect his own.

One important point never addressed in the early sources is
that up to the Spirit Lake massacre, Inkpaduta—the supposed
great hater of all whites, who was either forty-two or fifty-seven
years old depending on when one dates his birth—had never
killed a white and had only minor disputes with local settlers.
This historical evidence does not support the demonizing of Inkpaduta. The accusations made against him that have pervaded
whites' memory simply do not hold up.

A new interpretation of Inkpaduta's life—based not on myth,
legend, racism, or white memory but rather on sound historical
research—is long overdue. Such an approach, however, is not
easy to undertake. Most of what is written about Inkpaduta
comes from white sources. Inkpaduta has no papers, memoirs,
or letters to study; and after 1857 and the Spirit Lake massacre,
he was rarely seen by whites prior to his flight into Canada in
1877. This twenty-year gap in his life leaves many unanswered
questions. However, using the available sources, including accounts from Native Americans, one can examine Inkpaduta's
life from a new vantage point: not the traditional white view of
him as a savage, but a more balanced perspective of the Dakota
leader as a real human being influenced and shaped by his culture, the times he lived in, and his own personality.

Inkpaduta was not an evil man, but at times he showed poor
judgment and was hotheaded and impulsive. These traits led

him to commit violent acts. He was a man who loved his family and was loved by them and respected by many other Dakotas. Today, Inkpaduta is greatly honored and respected among the Dakotas and seen as a patriot who fought to protect his people. Rather than the bloodthirsty warrior of legend, Inkpaduta mostly wanted to be left alone. He remains a villain to whites primarily because, unlike Sitting Bull, Crazy Horse, and Little Crow, he was never caught, punished, or forced to surrender. Having never been forced onto a reservation, or beaten in battle, Inkpaduta could thus not be "redeemed" in the eyes of the whites. Inkpaduta, who never underwent any assimilation or conversion experience at the hands of whites, has forever retained the image of the feared "wild" American Indian who haunts the deep, dark regions of white America's psychological frontier. In the writings of most white historians, he still lurks there.

The life of Inkpaduta also serves as a symbol of the loss of independence and freedom for the great Sioux nation. Inkpaduta was present when the Dakotas in Minnesota were forced onto a reservation in the 1850s; he subsequently lived with the Yanktons and Yanktonais in the 1860s until white pressure forced them to surrender their autonomy. Finally, he supported the Lakotas in their struggle against the U.S. Army in the Great Sioux War and, after their defeat, fled to Canada with the remnants of the Sioux.

Inkpaduta is also important today because whites of the time thought he was: to frontier settlers and the military, he was for many years Public Enemy Number One. He became a bogeyman who terrified whites. Time and again the army sent out patrols to capture him, only to return empty handed. Inkpaduta's ability to elude capture, if for no other reason, makes his life worthy of study.

*Inkpaduta*

## CHAPTER 1

# "Such a Life as Almost All Boys Dream Of"

## THE WAHPEKUTES IN MINNESOTA

Minnesota may not be the place of origin of the Dakota or Sioux nation, but it is viewed as the tribe's traditional homeland. It is not certain when the Sioux first migrated into the area. However, by the mid–seventeenth century they were firmly established in Minnesota. The term *Dakota* means "friend" in the Siouan language. This term is apropos as the Dakota nation was more of an alliance than a unified nation. Over the next two hundred years, the Sioux would expand outside of Minnesota onto the northern plains and divide into three tribal divisions: Lakotas, Nakotas, and Dakotas. Each, in turn, subdivided into a number of bands and villages.

Prior to the great expansion to the west, seven bands or "council fires" dwelled in Minnesota: the Mdewakantons, Wahpetons, Sissetons, Wahpekutes, Yanktons, Yanktonais, and Tetons. The Tetons eventually became the Lakota division of the Sioux; the Yanktons and Yanktonais became the Nakota division, while the Mdewakantons, Wahpetons, Sissetons, and Wahpekutes made up the Dakota division, also known as the Santee.[1] The

Lakotas and Nakotas would leave Minnesota and develop plains-oriented cultures. The Dakotas stayed in the traditional homeland and remained more of a woodland culture similar to the Ojibwas, Potawatomis, and Ho-Chunks.

Scholars give various reasons for the westward migration of the Sioux. In part, this migration occurred in response to the Ojibwas moving into northern Minnesota and challenging Sioux hegemony in the region. In the 1730s and 1740s, the Ojibwas pushed inland from Lake Superior toward the Mille Lacs Lake region of northern Minnesota. For several decades the Sioux fought to hang on to the area before suffering key defeats in a series of battles in the mid-1700s. By the 1760s the better-armed Ojibwas were masters of the north.[2]

Yet, even before the Ojibwas advanced into Minnesota, the Sioux were pushing westward. More important than enemy pressure from the north were the white fur traders setting up for business on the Missouri River and diminishing animal resources in Minnesota. By 1830, in fact, buffalo were seldom seen in Minnesota. Trade and hunting, more than any other factors, caused the Lakotas and Nakotas to leave their traditional homeland. By the 1680s the Sioux had started to move westward. Within forty years they dominated the present-day states of South and North Dakota east of the Missouri River. In the 1750s the Lakotas crossed the Missouri and pushed even farther west. The Nakotas remained behind, east of the river on lands granted to them by the Lakotas.[3]

Having obtained horses and guns, the Lakotas were well prepared to continue advancing to the west. By 1776 they possessed all of present-day South Dakota and most of North Dakota. In the mid–eighteenth century, Lakota landholdings expanded farther into Montana, Wyoming, and Nebraska. In 1850 the thirteen bands of the Sioux claimed 80 million acres of land spread out between Montana and Minnesota. By this time, interaction between the Lakotas and the easternmost Sioux — the Dako-

tas—had lessened. Distance and different trade centers—the
Missouri River for the Lakotas and the Mississippi River for
the Dakotas—led each group to have little involvement with the
other.[4]

Considered the oldest division of the tribe, and thus much
respected by the other Sioux, the Dakota or Santee were also the
smallest division in numbers. Remaining behind in southern
Minnesota and northern Iowa, the Dakota mainly lived in semipermanent villages. The Sissetons and Wahpetons, referred to
by whites as the Upper Sioux, lived farthest to the west. They
kept in greater contact with the Lakotas and Nakotas and lived
along Big Stone Lake and Lake Traverse and inhabited a few
villages on the upper Minnesota River. The Mdewakantons, who
along with the Wahpekutes were called the Lower Sioux, were
spread out along the Mississippi and lower Minnesota Rivers.
The Wahpekutes were the smallest of the four bands, number-
ing fewer than one thousand people; they lived west of the
Mdewakantons along the headwaters of the Des Moines River
and the upper Cannon River near the Iowa border.[5]

Inkpaduta was born to a minor Wahpekute war chief in either
1800 or 1815. As with many of the events in Inkpaduta's life,
there is disagreement over his birth year. One group of writers,
including Lucius Hubbard and Return Holcombe, authors of
*Minnesota in Three Centuries, 1655–1908*, maintains that Inkpaduta was born in 1800 on the Cannon River. L.P. Lee, who in
1857 wrote the first book on the massacre, *History of the Spirit Lake
Massacre*, also believed Inkpaduta was born in that year.[6]

Doane Robinson disagreed with this early birth date for Inkpaduta; he believed Inkpaduta was born in 1815 along the Watonwan River near present-day St. James, Minnesota.[7] Given certain events in Inkpaduta's life, it would appear that Robinson is
probably correct. Specifically, it is known that Inkpaduta participated in the Battle of Killdeer Mountain in 1864; it is more
believable that an Inkpaduta in his late forties would still have

been an active warrior rather than a man in his mid-sixties. Conjecture aside, the age of Inkpaduta remains unknown.

Inkpaduta's father was Wamdisapa, or Black Eagle, a war chief of the village led by Shakeska (White Nails). Wamdisapa had two wives: one was a Mdewakanton, and the other, Inkpaduta's mother, was either a Wahpekute or a Sisseton. Inkpaduta likely was the eldest son with two sisters, one who later married a Sisseton chieftain and the other a Lakota, and at least one brother.[8] At birth, a Dakota child was given one of ten common names for boys or girls. The name for a firstborn male child was Chaska, and this may have been the name initially given to Inkpaduta. Later, after a ceremony at age three or four, he would have been given a more personal name. Finally, Inkpaduta would have received his final name as an adult. Inkpaduta's name has been translated to mean "Scarlet Point," "Scarlet or Red End," or "Scarlet at the Top." It has been said that his name was derived either from a red ornament placed in his hair as a child or from serious bleeding when he was circumcised.[9]

Among the Dakotas, child rearing was very important; it was marked by love and tenderness and only rare corporal punishment. Parents asked rather than commanded their children to obey. Inkpaduta's mother would have picked out a hero or man of great character from their family or band as a model to train her son. Both parents, other relatives, and friends helped teach Inkpaduta all he needed to know about life. He was taught not to cry at night so as to not give the village away to a lurking enemy. Inkpaduta learned that the world was dangerous; one could be attacked or killed at any time. Like other boys, Inkpaduta was taught how to be a warrior as well as a hunter and to learn patience, physical endurance, and courage along with a knowledge of weapons.[10]

Overall, life for a Dakota boy was one of fun and adventure. Charles Eastman, a Dakota Sioux, remembered his youth with fondness: "The Indian boy enjoyed such a life as almost all boys dream of and would choose for themselves if they were permitted to do so." It was a free outdoor life full of racing, wrestling, swimming, sham battles, and hunting small animals and birds with bows and arrows the boys made themselves.[11]

As Inkpaduta grew older, he was instructed in the folklore and history of the Dakotas, the morals and values of his people, and the extensive and somewhat confusing kinship bonds of the Sioux. The Dakotas had extremely close kinship bonds that extended to the most remote relatives. The term *Father* could apply to one's biological father, uncle, father's male cousin, or father's cross cousin. *Mother* could mean the birth mother, aunt, or cousin. When the Sioux used terms like father or children, they did not necessarily mean to denote a superior or inferior relationship. Rather, these terms reflected the custom of kinship bonding in which fathers and children owed each other various duties or obligations. All types of relatives were to be treated with kindness, generosity, and loyalty. Younger kinsmen were to defer to elder kinsmen. As Gary Clayton Anderson, author of *Kinsmen of Another Kind*, noted, "This unique communal understanding — a conscious regard for the safety and welfare of one's relatives, sharing, and a strong sense of native identity and superiority" — helped define the Sioux as a nation.[12] It also would play a role in Inkpaduta's ability to avoid capture by the army and successfully move from one division of the Sioux to another over his lifetime.

Dakota villages were mainly a kinship unit. Villages consisted of fifty to four hundred people and were economically self-sufficient. A village had a sense of landownership as a communal group. Its members would hunt and make war; take care of the needy, widows, and poor; and socialize together. Each village would have a peace and a war leader. Because of the kinship ties, individuals married persons from outside their village and with

A Sioux village on the Minnesota River. Inkpaduta's village would have been similar. Artist: Edwin Whitefield. Courtesy of the Minnesota Historical Society.

whom they did not share a common grandparent. There was not much polygamy among the Sioux, although it did occur more often among chieftains.[13]

The Dakota governmental system was very democratic, entailing a great deal of discussion and agreement of the majority before any decisions were reached. There was a council of elders and only two permanent offices: the head chief or peace chief, and the chief soldier or war chief. Unlike what many whites then and now assume, chiefs were not like kings with absolute power; they consulted with the people and elders, listening to their views before leading through their influence and respect. Over time, the position of head chief became hereditary, passed on usually, but not always, to the eldest son. Other relatives could and did at times challenge sons for control of the village. Such struggles for leadership could divide a village, causing it to break apart, and even lead to violence. The murder of a chief was not unknown.[14]

Friction also could exist between the head chief and the war chief. Jealousy often caused the bad relationships. War chiefs would rebel against the leadership of the head chief, causing the people of the village to take sides. If matters grew too difficult, the war chief would break off from the village with his supporters and form a new camp where he would be head chief.[15] Such a falling out occurred between Inkpaduta's father, Wamdisapa, and the head chief of their village.

Although there could be conflicts within a village, camp life was fairly harmonious with the Dakotas occupied with their usual daily tasks. The four Dakota bands lived in semipermanent villages. In the spring the men trapped; the women planted corn around the village before the camp broke into small groups and left to hunt for the summer, living in lodges made from buffalo hides. The Dakotas were heavy meat eaters, consuming muskrat, gopher, squirrel, duck, goose, elk, bear, and fish. However, the main meat sources were buffalo, especially for the upper bands of the Sissetons and Wahpetons, and deer, more common among the lower bands of the Mdewakantons and Wahpekutes. The women would also gather wild vegetables, nuts, and berries.[16] In the fall the scattered groups would gather again at the main village to harvest corn and rice before leaving on a fall deer hunt; they then returned to spend the winter in the village.

There were some differences among the four Dakota bands. The Sissetons and Wahpetons, living farther to the west, kept better contact and closer relations with the Yankton and Lakota Sioux, hunted buffalo, and were more nomadic than the lower bands. The Mdewakantons and Wahpekutes continued to harvest subsistence foods like rice and corn, hunted deer, and lived in more permanent villages. Still, the four bands were close, often intermixing, intermarrying, hunting, warring, and socializing together.[17]

The Dakotas' population, never large, fluctuated over time but remained fairly constant. In 1823 their numbers were estimated to be around 5,700 but fell to fewer than 4,000 in 1839, before rising again to roughly 6,000 by 1850.[18] The Dakotas held extensive lands for such a small tribe, in what would be Minnesota, Iowa, Wisconsin, and North and South Dakota. They lived on lands that were picturesque and pleasant, a mixture of woods and prairies, dotted with numerous lakes and tree-lined streams and rivers. One early white visitor described the region as "gently rolling prairie, occasionally interrupted by a small patch or thin line of timber indicative of a lake or water course."[19]

In this beautiful region living among his people, the Wahpekutes, Inkpaduta matured into a man. Although he would have experienced the carefree life of a boy, with the annual hunting, trapping, and gathering cycles, and the usual harmony of village life among the Dakotas, Inkpaduta was also aware of the great changes that were affecting his people by the early nineteenth century. Four factors were beginning to put great pressure on the traditional lives of the Dakotas. White encroachment, reduc-

tion of food sources, disease, and intertribal warfare were forcing change.

The French were the first Europeans to become acquainted
with the Dakotas. In the mid–seventeenth century French missionaries and fur traders traveled into Minnesota. They set up
relations with the Dakotas that remained strong until the 1763
French defeat in the French and Indian War. Soon after, British
fur traders moved into the area and established economic ties.
By 1800 the Dakotas had become economically dependent on
the trade goods of the Europeans.[20]

Following the Louisiana Purchase in 1803, the Americans arrived. The first official contact came with the Lewis and Clark
military expedition up the Missouri River. In the summer of
1804, Meriwether Lewis and William Clark met with leaders of
the Yankton and Lakota Sioux, getting them to recognize U.S.
supremacy over the region. In 1805 Zebulon Pike led another
army expedition up the Mississippi River into Minnesota. In September Pike signed a treaty with leaders of the Dakotas, purchasing two tracts of land as sites for possible military forts. Pike paid
only two hundred dollars' worth of goods and liquor with a
promise of another two thousand dollars for more than one
hundred thousand acres of land. This set the stage for subsequent swindling of the Dakotas by other government officials.[21]

In 1819, following the War of 1812 (during which the Dakotas
favored the British), the American army established Fort Snelling in Minnesota. The army was soon followed by American fur
traders (who replaced the British traders), missionaries, and an
Indian agent for the region. The American fur traders continued to deepen the economic dependence of the Dakotas,
while the missionaries challenged the Sioux's traditional religious beliefs and sense of cultural identity. In 1820 Lawrence
Taliaferro arrived at Fort Snelling to take up his duties as Indian
agent for the nearby St. Peter Agency.[22]

The second pressure came along with the Americans. The

desire of white fur traders to obtain as much fur as possible, coupled with the Dakotas' growing addiction to European/American goods, led to a sharp decline in the animal food supply by the 1820s. By the mid-1830s the buffalo had disappeared along the Minnesota River and could only be hunted increasingly farther to the west, and small game, other than muskrats, became harder to find. Also by the 1830s, the fur trade collapsed just as the Dakotas were finding it difficult to feed their families from hunting. Most game was now gone from the Sisseton and Wahpeton lands, while the Mdewakantons and Wahpekutes were even more desperate, with virtually no animals available in their territories for trade or food.[23]

A third pressure coming from contact with whites were such diseases as smallpox, cholera, and whooping cough. In 1836 the Dakotas were hit hard by a smallpox outbreak, which accounted for the drop in population they experienced in the 1830s.[24] One of those affected by the epidemic was Inkpaduta. Numerous eyewitness accounts describe the pockmarked scars on his face inflicted by smallpox.

The fourth and final pressure came from two long-term and destructive tribal wars with the Ojibwas and with the Sac and Fox. The Sioux were a warrior people, as clearly exhibited by their conquest of the northern plains. As a young boy, Inkpaduta would have been taught how to be a warrior and to make war on his people's enemies. To the Dakotas, all war was defensive. One fought to protect the tribe's lands, stop trespassers, or avenge an attack upon one's people. Revenge raids were most common, with all people — women and children included — fair game in an attack.[25]

Samuel Pond, an early Christian missionary to the Sioux, witnessed Dakota war parties, noting that they were "generally small and composed chiefly of very young men, while most of the men were engaged in other pursuits." When a war party returned to its village after a successful revenge raid, the people would run out to the warriors rejoicing in the victory over their enemy and a debt repaid. A scalp dance would commonly follow the return. Both men and women would participate with drums beating rhythm and songs expressing a tone of triumph. The dance could last deep into the night.[26]

The ongoing war with the Ojibwas was the most critical to the Dakotas. By the 1820s the conflict had lasted for almost a century. It had not gone well for the Dakotas. The Ojibwas boasted they had driven their enemy out of northern Minnesota, and by the 1790s even the Dakotas accepted the loss of this region forever.[27]

But for Inkpaduta and the Wahpekutes, the war with the Sac and Fox truly was a life-or-death struggle. At stake were the important hunting grounds in northern Iowa. In the later seventeenth century, under pressure from the aggressive Iroquois, the Sac and Fox began to move westward. By 1766 they had passed through Wisconsin and settled in villages along the Mississippi, Rock and Wisconsin Rivers in Illinois and Iowa.[28] From there they challenged the Dakotas for control of prime hunting and trapping areas. By fighting the Sac and Fox, Inkpaduta became a successful and noted warrior. White writers would use this as the basis for branding Inkpaduta and his father as evil men, whose love of war would threaten the very survival of the Wahpekutes and lead to two brutal murders.

CHAPTER 2

# *"Everything was Destroyed"*

## WAMDISAPA AND THE SAC AND FOX WARS

White writers' first negative depictions of Inkpaduta emerge from the warfare between the Dakotas and the Sac and Fox and other events stemming from that conflict, especially in the 1830s and 1840s. As warfare with the Sac and Fox reached a critical level for the Wahpekutes in the 1820s, while Inkpaduta was still a child, it was his father Wamdisapa whom white writers first accused of having an evil, violent character.

Numerous writers have blamed Wamdisapa for the continual warfare with the Sac and Fox that was pushing the Wahpekutes toward extinction. Writers related how Tasagi, the noble leader of the Cannon River Wahpekutes, and head chief of Wamdisapa's village, desired peace with the Sac and Fox to save his people; however, the warlike and treacherous Wamdisapa refused his wise council and broke off to form his own camp of malcontents. According to many writers, Wamdisapa, Inkpaduta, or both men later murdered the peaceable Tasagi, causing Wamdisapa and his followers to become renegades in the eyes of other Dakotas.[1] Upon the death of Tasagi, his son, Wamundeyakapi, became chief. He too was murdered, along with seventeen other Wahpekute men by a jealous and vengeful Inkpaduta.[2] In fact, so bloodthirsty had Inkpaduta become that he was also the alleged murderer of Wamdisapa, his own father.[3]

White writers used only the most negative terms to describe Wamdisapa. Doane Robinson said he had a violent and "fiendish temper" and "cruel instincts." Frank Herriot, a historian for the Minnesota Historical Society in the 1930s, described Wamdisapa as "contentious and irreconcilable . . . arrogant and brutal in temperament." A later historian, Michael Clodfelter, wrote that Inkpaduta was "almost demented" and accused Wamdisapa of teaching him his evil ways, calling him a "chief of violent temper and villainous character."[4] Although little of the above statements about Wamdisapa or his son is accurate, it is true that Inkpaduta grew up during a period of crisis for the Wahpekutes.

Perhaps one reason the initial negative opinions of Wamdisapa and Inkpaduta arose is because they were Wahpekutes. The Wahpekutes were not held in high regard by the incoming whites. Zebulon Pike believed the tribe was composed of individuals kicked out of the other Dakota bands and wrote, "They appeared to me to be the most stupid and inactive of all the Sioux." A later military explorer, Stephen Long, agreed with Pike, calling the Wahpekutes "lawless." Local traders such as Joseph Renville and white settlers like Harvey Ingham also disapproved of the Wahpekutes. Ingham claimed they "were the meanest and most worthless of all the Dakotas."[5] While it is unclear why the Wahpekutes had such a bad reputation, it may have come partly from their habit of raiding boats belonging to traders on the Mississippi River.[6]

The Wahpekutes, whose name means "Shooters Among the Leaves," were fairly nomadic in the area around the Cannon River, their main hunting grounds near present-day Fairbault, Minnesota. They were said to be the first Dakota band to obtain firearms and push into northern Iowa. Here the very indepen-

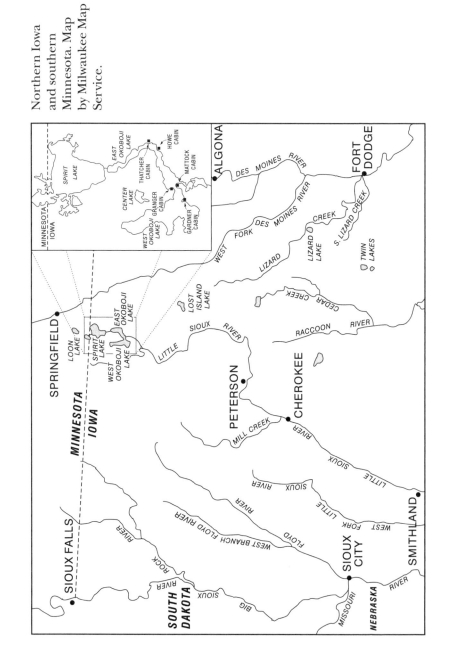

Northern Iowa and southern Minnesota. Map by Milwaukee Map Service.

dent, loosely grouped Wahpekutes were challenged by tribes like the Iowas, Potawatomis, Ho-Chunk, and the Sac and Fox.[7] The Wahpekutes' conflict with the Sac and Fox centered on control of the region around the headwaters of the Des Moines River. The ensuing warfare was nearly constant and caused havoc for the population of the Wahpekutes.

Never a large band, the Wahpekutes at one time numbered as many as nine hundred to a thousand people. But by the early to mid–nineteenth century their population had fallen to around five hundred to six hundred.[8] Following the War of 1812, the Wahpekutes suffered such losses that French Crow, a head chief of the band, lost favor with his people and was replaced by White Nails. When White Nails died in 1822, his son, Tasagi (His Crane), became the new head chief of the Cannon River Wahpe- kutes. Tasagi was young and inexperienced while Wamdisapa, perhaps either his cousin or nephew, already was an experienced war chief of the village.[9]

Missionary Stephen Riggs, who knew Wamdisapa later in his life, described him as stern and not very genial. Riggs did not care for his begging or how Wamdisapa's followers stole much of the minister's livestock, but he did admit that when his brother- in-law, Thomas Longley, drowned, Wamdisapa came to comfort Riggs and share his loss. Another settler, Martha Thorne, re- membered Wamdisapa as a kind man who "used to hold my little girl and measure her foot for moccasins. Then he would bring her the finest they could make and would be so pleased when they fitted." Descendants of Wamdisapa considered him to be a good man who tried to do what was right for his people and live in peace.[10]

From 1822 to 1825, Tasagi and Wamdisapa continued the war with the Sac and Fox. Indian Agent Lawrence Taliaferro noted in his journal the seriousness of the conflict and that since 1815 the Dakotas had lost 170 people in the fighting. Frustrated by the warfare, Taliaferro tried to mediate peace between the tribes.[11]

In 1825 he gained some success when a council, hosted by the U.S. government, was held at Prairie du Chien in Wisconsin.

Government agents hoped to end the warfare between the Ojibwas and Dakotas in the north and the Dakotas and Sac and Fox in the south by setting up tribal boundaries. Article I of a new Treaty of Prairie du Chien called for "perpetual peace" between the tribes. The document also attempted to establish a new tribal border from the mouth of the upper Iowa River southwest to the upper or second fork of the Des Moines River; the Dakotas were to live north of this border, and the Sac and Fox to the south. Almost immediately there was a dispute between the Wahpekutes and Sac and Fox over the location of the dividing line. The Wahpekutes believed the second fork of the Des Moines River was the Raccoon River but the Sac and Fox disagreed. This dispute left unclear who controlled lands in northern Iowa. Tasagi was one of the Wahpekute leaders who supported the Dakota view of the border but did sign the treaty in February 1826.[12]

For three years Tasagi, Wamdisapa, and the Wahpekutes kept the peace with the Sac and Fox. However, by early 1828 the Sac and Fox had resumed raiding the Dakotas. In February and March different groups of Dakotas were attacked by mounted Sac and Fox war parties. On November 15, 1828, Morgan, a war chief of the Sac and Fox, struck Tasagi's village near the Des Moines River. Most of the men, including Wamdisapa and Inkpaduta, were away hunting and returned to find a massacre. Wamdisapa later said, "I left my family, as I thought in safety, and went out to trap a little for myself, but on my return to my lodge, everything was destroyed." One of his wives, not Inkpaduta's mother, was dead, her head cut off and her body torn to pieces and thrown into the river. Tasagi's stepdaughter and grandchild were taken prisoner.[13] Although often accused of refusing to stop fighting the Sac and Fox, Wamdisapa had kept the peace for several years until this devastating personal loss. Wamdisapa, now angry with Tasagi, blamed him for signing the Treaty of Prairie du Chien and the resulting attacks by the Sac and Fox.[14]

The attack on their village and further raids eventually caused both Wamdisapa and Tasagi to resume the conflict with their old enemy. Also motivating their return to war was the need to protect dwindling food sources. With diminished wild game for food and trade, the Wahpekutes were forced to fight for control of northern Iowa. The Wahpekutes grew more economically dependent on the white traders, who wanted more furs from the Dakotas — something that did not please Wamdisapa. The traders, argued Wamdisapa, "wish to push us into the jaws of our enemies, and on dangerous ground, to get skins to pay our credit." In order to feed his people and keep obtaining necessary goods from the traders, Wamdisapa, who still had not retaliated against the Sac and Fox by July 1829, went back to war. At stake were the hunting grounds of the disputed northern Iowa region.[15] Nothing in his actions indicates a man obsessed with war or recklessly determined to fight no matter what may happen to his people. Simply stated, Wamdisapa resumed fighting to avenge his wife and to secure needed hunting grounds. These represent two common reasons for Dakota warfare.

Back at war with the Sac and Fox, both Tasagi and Wamdisapa turned to the Americans for support and aid in ending the conflict. On more than one occasion Tasagi journeyed to Fort Snelling to speak with Agent Taliaferro. Tasagi informed Taliaferro of the Sac and Fox raids and the renewed warfare between the tribes. Tasagi had hoped that the Treaty of Prairie du Chien would have ended the fighting, but he insisted the Wahpekutes had kept the peace until attacked by the Sac and Fox. He also spoke of the difficult economic conditions of the Cannon River Wahpekutes; his people were starving, unable to pay their debts to the traders because the war interrupted their hunting and trapping.[16] At no time did Tasagi blame Wamdisapa for the fighting; neither did Taliaferro in his daily journal.

It was clear Taliaferro believed that the Sac and Fox, especially Morgan, were responsible for the renewed conflict. He called the Wahpekutes an "unfortunate people" and expressed his belief that the Dakotas and Sac and Fox would continue fighting "as long as there is a *Brave* of either nation in existence." Alexander Ramsey, later territorial governor of Minnesota, agreed with Taliaferro about the cause for the warfare. Ramsey noted the Wahpekutes had to "bear the brunt of the enemies of their nation" to the south.[17]

Growing frustrated with Tasagi's leadership, Wamdisapa came to see Taliaferro in April 1829. After receiving many gifts and presents, Wamdisapa the war chief told Taliaferro that he had found his wife dismembered and thrown into the river "like the skin of a slaughtered deer" and that he had not yet led a revenge raid against his enemies. He blamed the traders for the warfare as they demanded more furs to pay off old debts, thus forcing the Wahpekutes to fight the Sac and Fox. Finally, Wamdisapa wanted to know what the Indian agent was going to do about the conflict, and why the U.S. Army had not arrested his wife's murderers.[18] Taliaferro did not indicate in his journal what his response was to Wamdisapa.

Later that summer, Wamdisapa planned a revenge raid. Joined by the Sissetons, Wamdisapa and his war party struck a lone lodge of Sac and Fox, killing several people.[19] His wife's murder had been avenged according to Dakota custom. Soon after this raid, the first reference to Inkpaduta emerges in Taliaferro's journal. On September 8, 1829, Taliaferro wrote that Wamdisapa's "son called to see me." This reference might not be to Inkpaduta, but given that Inkpaduta was likely Wamdisapa's eldest son, it probably is. The son talked with Taliaferro about the Wahpekutes' troubles with the Sac and Fox, again showing a desire for American aid in ending the warfare.[20]

Having failed once to stop the fighting, in 1830 the federal government tried again with another conference and treaty at

Prairie du Chien. This time, a forty-mile neutral zone was created in northern Iowa, carved from lands held by both the Dakotas and the Sac and Fox. It was hoped that such a neutral zone
would keep the two tribes apart and cause the warfare to cease.
In July nine Wahpekute chiefs signed another Treaty of Prairie
du Chien; the signers included neither Tasagi nor Wamdisapa.[21]
In August Tasagi and Wamdisapa went to Fort Snelling and met
with Taliaferro. Taliaferro explained the treaty to them and how
it would stop the warfare with the Sac and Fox. Both Wahpekute
leaders were dubious that the treaty would solve anything but
stated that they hoped it would.[22] It was probably this underlying
doubt toward the effectiveness of the treaty that led the two men
not to sign the document in the first place. If so, they were soon
proven right.

Within days after the treaty was signed, a Sac and Fox war
party crossed the neutral zone and attacked Wamdisapa's camp,
killing two men. Moreover, the U.S. government did not improve the situation when it moved a new tribe into the neutral
zone. As a condition of the 1830 Indian Removal Act, the Ho-
Chunks were moved into this area of Iowa. Soon this hapless
tribe was being attacked by both the Dakotas and the Sac and
Fox.[23] The new treaty had failed to end the fighting, and government actions further exacerbated the situation by introducing a
third tribe.

During the early 1830s, relations between Tasagi and Wamdisapa continued to worsen. It appears that Wamdisapa was los-
ing confidence in Tasagi's leadership abilities. The two men did
continue to work together when necessary. They often traveled
together to meet with Taliaferro, and both signed the 1836
treaty, along with other Dakota leaders, giving up rights to lands
in southwest Iowa and northwest Missouri. Also in 1836, both
leaders fought in Black Hawk's War supporting the U.S. Army
against their old enemy, the Sac and Fox.[24]

The background of Black Hawk's War is traceable to the late

1820s. Using a seriously flawed 1804 treaty signed by the Sac and
Fox, the federal government moved the tribe from its homelands in Illinois across the Mississippi River into Iowa. In 1832
Black Hawk led part of the tribe back into Illinois, claiming that
the lands still belonged to his people and hoping he could form
an alliance with tribes still dwelling there. His attempt at an
Indian alliance to stop white encroachment failed and led to the
conflict that bears his name. Chased by local militias and regular
army troops, Black Hawk tried desperately to evade his pursuers
and get his people back across the Mississippi. On August 1 the
Sac and Fox tried to cross the river at the mouth of the Bad Axe
River. Here they were caught by the U.S. Army, which attacked
them from the east side of the river and from a gunboat sail-
ing up the Mississippi. The slaughter was great; many survivors
reached the west bank of the river only to be killed by the Dakotas who came to fight their enemy.

Following their involvement in the Black Hawk's War, Wamdisapa had clearly broken with Tasagi by the mid-1830s, splitting
the Cannon River Wahpekutes and forming a new village with
himself as head chief. Tasagi and his supporters stayed along the
Cannon River while Wamdisapa moved his smaller village of sixty
to one hundred people to the Blue Earth River in Minnesota.[25]
From there he lived a nomadic life, doing a little planting of corn
but primarily hunting. It is stated that the cause for the split was
Tasagi's desire for peace and Wamdisapa's demand for war. This
does not seem likely, as neither man actively sought war and both
continued to raid the Sac and Fox after they parted.

The late 1830s proved to be a difficult period for the Wahpekutes. In 1837 a devastating smallpox epidemic struck the tribe.
Wamdisapa's village was hit hard—with only ten lodges and
fourteen warriors surviving the disease. Inkpaduta was among
those that survived, but he was badly scarred.[26] Aside from disease, hunger was a growing problem, forcing villages to become
smaller in order to obtain enough food. In 1838 traders made

the Wahpekutes' living situation more dangerous by refusing to extend any further credit to the Dakotas until they paid their debts. Needing furs to trade, the Dakotas, including the Wahpekutes, pushed into lands held by the Sac and Fox. This caused increased warfare and death.[27]

Due to the effects of warfare and disease, the Wahpekutes numbered only 325 people by 1839. Fewer than one hundred tribe members would have been men able to fight and hunt for the tribe. Taliaferro noted the Wahpekutes were being wiped out. In June 1839 Tasagi visited the Indian agent. He complained of renewed Sac and Fox attacks and blamed Taliaferro for not stopping the war. "It is your fault," accused Tasagi, "You advised us to keep the peace — we have done so — The result is by listening to you . . . we are now almost destroyed."[28] Once again, Tasagi did not blame Wamdisapa for the continuing conflict with the Sac and Fox.

In 1841 Tasagi and Wamdisapa again came together to sign another treaty, the never enacted Doty Treaty. Conditions had become so difficult for the Dakotas that leaders from the four bands signed the Doty Treaty, which would have ceded all their lands in Minnesota and Iowa — 30 million acres except for 70,000 acres along the Minnesota River. This was in return for support from the federal government to help the tribes establish new lives based on assimilation and citizenship. Sometime prior to the treaty signing, Wamdisapa had moved his village, now known as the Red Top band, to the Vermillion River in South Dakota. The size of the village varied from as few as five lodges to as many as eighty. Having moved so far away from the rest of the Wahpekutes, the Red Top band (including Inkpaduta who went with his father) began interacting socially and politically with the Yanktons and Sissetons.[29] This voluntary removal from the other Wahpekutes has led writers to claim that Wamdisapa and his followers were renegades unwanted by the Dakotas, but there is no evidence of this rejection.

There is also no evidence that Wamdisapa or Inkpaduta had any part in the murder of Tasagi, which is the chief reason writers cite for why Wamdisapa became a renegade who fled to the Vermillion River. In 1842, soon after the signing of the Doty Treaty, Tasagi was murdered. It was not uncommon for a chief to be murdered by a member of his village; a Wahpekute named Wood Breaker most likely killed Tasagi, for an unknown reason.[30] Living hundreds of miles away, neither Wamdisapa nor Inkpaduta were responsible. Neither man had a reason to murder Tasagi. Wamdisapa had established his own village years earlier, and since then he had cooperated with Tasagi on several occasions. Warfare with the Sac and Fox was no longer a major issue because in 1842 the tribe had signed a treaty giving up their lands in Iowa. In 1845 the Sac and Fox were to be moved farther west by the federal government.

Throughout the early 1840s Wamdisapa and his followers continued to live along the Vermillion River. The size of Wamdisapa's village varied as other non-Wahpekute Dakotas joined up with the aging chief. Whites since have maintained that the people who attached themselves to the Red Top band were outlaws and renegades from other bands. Thomas Hughes, an early-twentieth-century writer, called them "a gang of savage free-booters." Another writer from the same period said they gloried "in the fact that their crimes were a camp-fire horror in every tepee from Iowa to Canada."[31] But Wamdisapa was not a renegade; the four bands of the Dakotas intermixed with the Red Top band, the band virtually merged with the Sissetons, and it does not appear that Wamdisapa's followers were as evil as later portrayed.

There is at least one instance when Wamdisapa was asked to rein in his young men. At Fort Vermillion, Father Pierre-Jean De Smet, the famed Catholic missionary, met with Wamdisapa and asked him to stop his people's horse raids against the Potawatomis. Wamdisapa was friendly and outgoing with the priest, but the raids continued.[32]

Besides some raiding against traditional enemies, Wamdisapa's Wahpekutes lived a fairly quiet life along the Vermillion. At one point, the chief received from the Indian agent at Fort Vermillion a small annuity from the 1830 Prairie du Chien sale of Dakota lands, even though he never personally signed the treaty.[33]

During this time Inkpaduta emerged from the shadow of his father and became a mature man. Descriptions of Inkpaduta frequently comment on the same physical features. He was six feet tall — tall even for the Dakotas — stout, with broad shoulders and a powerful frame. His face was long and narrow with deep-set "black sparkling eyes," high nose, and large mouth. Most obvious were the smallpox scars on his face and his nearsighted "squinty" eyes. Inkpaduta's failing vision would eventually cause him to be virtually blind later in his life.[34]

It is partly from Inkpaduta's physical appearance that whites could envision him as an evil figure. He was not a handsome man. Settlers who saw Inkpaduta found his appearance "revolting" and "repulsive." D.C. Evans, a former Minnesota state senator from Mankato, remembered Inkpaduta's "ugly, vicious look." G.Wallace Adams from Smithland, Iowa, described him as morose and sullen. Joseph Taylor stated that "his whole make-up had the showing of a humble, ill-used mendicant."[35] Inkpaduta's appearance clearly made it easier for settlers to see him as ominous and dangerous, an enemy to be feared and distrusted.

Looking past the physical, the Dakotas and some whites remembered Inkpaduta more positively. To them, Inkpaduta was a soft-spoken, quiet man. He was a successful warrior against the Sac and Fox, Omahas, and Potawatomis — courageous, zealous, and capable of enduring hardships. He was admired for how he remained true to the traditions of his people and how he lived harmoniously with nature. Inkpaduta was known to be intelligent, honest, and a good hunter. By all accounts, Inkpaduta was kind and gentle toward his family. According to Curtis Lamb, an early settler in Iowa, Inkpaduta hated alcohol, because he lost a brother in a drunken fight with another Dakota and because it made his men angry, which led to trouble.[36]

Charles Eastman remembered the great impression that Inkpaduta made on him as a young boy because of "his personality and character." He added, "I found that Inkpaduta was not a bad man. According to Indian customs and usages he commanded a very high respect from all of the tribes. He was a man of considerable mental gifts and force." J.F. Waggoner, a Dakota woman who knew Inkpaduta's sister, believed that "to say that Inkpaduta was a wiley [*sic*] rascal and a murderous sneak is not saying the truth about him. Inkpaduta was a patriot, or considered so by his band." Old Bull, a Lakota Sioux, recalled Inkpaduta as one of the "bravest and most courageous warriors they [the Wahpekutes] had." Ambrose Little Ghost, a great-grandson, states that the family has always remembered Inkpaduta as a good father who was helpful and concerned about the welfare of his people. Mrs. Arthur Young, another descendant of Inkpaduta's, insisted, "If he was a bad man, you can bet it was white men who pushed him to his bad deeds." Inkpaduta's sister felt much the same way, remembering her brother as a humble man who wanted to avoid trouble when possible. Yet, when pushed or insulted, he could have a violent temper that could make Inkpaduta "do things to the extreme. Then the innocent had to suffer with the guilty."[37] This dangerous temper was a serious character flaw, and it led Inkpaduta to commit a brutal massacre, thus sealing his fate, in the eyes of whites, as an enemy.

Not all whites saw Inkpaduta negatively. Two traders, Martin McLeod and Curtis Lamb, thought very highly of him. Lamb was the second settler to move into what would later be Woodbury County, Iowa. He defended Inkpaduta as honest and trustwor-

thy, so much so that Lamb asked him to watch over his family
when he was away on business. Inkpaduta later taught Lamb how
to speak Sioux and often played with his children.[38]

Inkpaduta had a number of children with his multiple wives.
He married young and produced children well into his late sixties. Eastman claims he had as many as ten sons and ten daughters. Among his children were two sets of twin boys. The older
twins were Mo-co-aque-mon (Roaring Cloud) and Mo-co-po-
co (Fire Cloud). Makamahedmane (Sounds The Ground As
He Walks) and Oyemakasan (Tracking White Earth) were the
younger twins, born sometime prior to the Spirit Lake massacre.
Big Face, Little Ghost, and Charley Maku were other sons, and
additional sons may have included Thunder Cloud and Walks
Under the Ground. All of his older sons were said to be able warriors, while Roaring Cloud had a fondness for trinkets, earrings,
arm bands, and red leggings; Fire Cloud enjoyed footracing and
making trades. Inkpaduta's children loved and respected their
father, who treated them well. Today, the numerous descendants
of Inkpaduta are scattered out across the northern plains and
into Canada.[39]

Since Inkpaduta was himself apparently such a good (and
prolific) father, it is surprising that later writers accused him of
patricide. Again, evidence does not bear out this claim. Sometime in the mid-1840s Wamdisapa moved his village back to Minnesota and settled near present-day St. Peter. In the summer of
1846 Reverend Stephen Riggs came to visit the ailing chief. Riggs
reported that soon after his visit Wamdisapa died, presumably
from his illness. He makes no mention of murder or of Inkpaduta having anything to do with the death of his father.[40]

Inkpaduta has also been accused of another murder, the killing of Wamundeyakapi. Following the murder of Tasagi, his son,
Wamundeyakapi, became the new head chief of the Cannon
River Wahpekutes. Although he was not Tasagi's eldest son, Wamundeyakapi was handsome, intelligent, and well suited to lead

his people. He had been chief for eight years when, in July 1849, he and seventeen followers were murdered in their sleep while hunting near the headwaters of the Des Moines River near Bear Lakes in Minnesota. Inkpaduta has long been blamed for the murders. Reasons proffered for why he would kill Wamundeya-kapi are confusing, being often tied to the myth that Inkpaduta or Wamdisapa had killed Tasagi and were exiled from the Wah-pekutes. Building off this premise, writers claimed Inkpaduta was jealous of Wamundeyakapi and wanted revenge for being exiled. Furthermore, writers added that Inkpaduta murdered the eighteen fellow Wahpekutes just for the love of killing.[41]

Alexander Ramsey, the territorial governor of Minnesota, at first believed that Inkpaduta was guilty of the massacre. So did many Sissetons and Wahpetons who had heard he committed the murders. Later, Ramsey learned the truth. In a report to the Commissioner of Indian Affairs, Ramsey wrote, "The offenders in the affair belong to the Fox tribe of Indians" and added that "justice and policy alike demand that adequate reparations be exacted from the tribe." The accuracy of Ramsey's report was borne out when the U.S. government promised to pay compensation to the Wahpekutes for the murders. The claim was later brought up at the 1851 treaty conference at Mendota, Minnesota, when Wahpekute leaders requested the compensation money due them for the Sac and Fox slaughter of their people be paid.[42]

Because Wamdisapa, and later Inkpaduta, broke from the Cannon River Wahpekutes and settled far away to the west, many people—both American Indians and whites—have come to believe that father and son became renegades following the murder of their fellow Wahpekutes. The Dakotas took murder seriously, allowing several different recourses for punishment of the murderer. Relatives of the victim could start a blood feud with the murderer and seek revenge. If it was believed that the victim had been killed by accident or that the murder was not premeditated, the murderer could compensate the family of the victim with costly gifts. Often, the murderer was driven into exile from the village.[43] The historical confusion over the deaths of Tasagi, Wamundeyakapi, and Wamdisapa, coupled with the Red Top band's move to South Dakota, led many, both then and now, to brand Inkpaduta a renegade Wahpekute exiled for his crimes.

Writing about the massacre at Spirit Lake, L. P. Lee stated Inkpaduta was a renegade and the leader of an outlaw band of Sioux known for their "continual depredations on the whites" and "shocking barbarities." A "smallpox-scarred Wahpekute renegade" is how Michael Clodfelter described him. Even Inkpaduta's niece assumed he was a renegade, believing "the isolation of Inkpaduta was self-imposed. It was a confession of his guilt in killing Wamundeyakapi." Only Charles Eastman maintained that Inkpaduta was not a renegade, explaining that Dakota bands were known for their independence and that Inkpaduta and his father had simply broken away from the Wahpekutes to form a new village.[44]

As neither Wamdisapa nor Inkpaduta had committed murder, there was no blood feud with the relatives of the victims or compensation to be paid, and exile was unnecessary. They were not renegades as popularly portrayed; however, it is clear that Inkpaduta was starting to be viewed as a renegade regardless of the truth, and events following his father's death would only add to this belief.

CHAPTER 3

# "Our Prairies are Settling up Rapidly"

SINTOMINIDUTA AND THE WHITE
SETTLEMENT OF IOWA

The decade following Wamdisapa's death brought increasing change and difficulties for the Dakotas. Already facing
diminishing big game and trapping resources, costly intertribal
warfare, and devastating disease, by the late 1840s the Dakotas
were faced with ever-increasing numbers of white settlers moving into Minnesota and Iowa and new pressures from the federal
government to sell their lands and move onto a reservation
where assimilation efforts would only intensify. The incoming
settlers arrived with cultural and social values often at odds with
those of the Dakotas. Disagreements and conflicting views over
landownership and use of local resources added to tensions on
the frontier.

For Inkpaduta, it was a time of further isolation from the
Wahpekutes, as the main band would soon sign over tribal lands
to the U.S. government and move onto a reservation. Inkpaduta
preferred to remain nomadic and free; he did not agree with the
land sale. His efforts to retain the traditional lifestyle of his people put him at odds with settlers occupying lands in northern

Iowa that were vacant after the removal of the Sac and Fox. The lands that the whites settled on included the Spirit Lake region, an area of spiritual importance to the Dakotas.

In his self-published biography of Inkpaduta, Maxwell Van Nuys contends that Inkpaduta was a gifted and skilled leader who, time and again, forged alliances among the Sioux to continue his unending vendetta against whites. It is more likely, however, that Inkpaduta, although a competent warrior, was not a very effective leader—so much so that he failed to become chief of the Red Top band upon Wamdisapa's death.

Being the son of Wamdisapa made Inkpaduta a logical choice to replace his father as the next chief. But the band began to fragment after Wamdisapa's death, with many members apparently not accepting Inkpaduta as leader. Instead, Sintominiduta (All Over Red) became the new chief. Sintominiduta, a Sisseton, was originally a member of Sleepy Eye's village, who may have been his father-in-law, before leaving the camp after possibly committing a murder. Along with a group of Sisseton followers who went with him, Sintominiduta's village initially became known as the Little Rock band. This group fought several battles with the Potawatomis in northeastern Iowa, including an ambush of a chief named Old Lizard in present-day Webster County. After several years Sintominiduta's Little Rock band merged with Wamdisapa's Red Top band.[1]

There is disagreement over Sintominiduta's relationship with Inkpaduta. Numerous sources, including contemporary newspaper accounts and current Internet sites, state that Inkpaduta and Sintominiduta were brothers. William Williams, the post sutler at Fort Dodge, knew both men and claimed this assessment was factual. Frank Herriot, Harvey Ingham, and Thomas Hughes, later writers dealing with this period of history, stated Sintominiduta and Inkpaduta were siblings. This is also the standard opinion of the Dakotas today.[2]

Other sources maintain that Sintominiduta was Inkpaduta's

brother-in-law, having married one of Wamdisapa's daughters. But J. Waggoner, herself a Dakota who knew Inkpaduta's family, believed the two men were not brothers but cousins; the kinship terms among the Dakotas whereby cousins call each other "brother" had led whites to misinterpret the relationship of Sintominiduta and Inkpaduta.[3] Thus, when Inkpaduta referred to Sintominiduta as his brother, whites took the term at face value rather than understand the Sioux kinship definition. It is most likely the men were not brothers but were, in some way, related by kinship.

Much like Inkpaduta, Sintominiduta was a well-built, tall man. A Mankato settler who met him described the chief as "a magnificent specimen physically — over six feet tall and finely proportioned. . . . He had a large intellectual looking head, large eyes, with an abundance of glossy black hair." Sintominiduta at times dressed like a white man, and D.C. Evans said he resembled Henry Clay.[4]

Regardless of how Sintominiduta became chief, Inkpaduta did not seem envious of Sintominiduta position. Inkpaduta remained in the diminished Red Top band as a subchief to Sintominiduta. Periodically, Inkpaduta and a few close followers would leave the band to hunt or trap before returning to the main village.[5] As he journeyed through southern Minnesota and northern Iowa, Inkpaduta could see a new threat to his independence and nomadic lifestyle emerging from the expansion of white settlement in the area.

The 1840s and 1850s epitomized the era of Manifest Destiny. It was a time of nationalistic patriotism and westward expansion. The idea that the United States was destined to be a great nation, expanding from sea to sea and perhaps even farther, took hold among the majority white population. American Indians and Mexicans would have to stand aside as white Americans fulfilled God's plan to award them ownership of as much land as they needed. Jingoistic and racist, this belief in Manifest Destiny pushed settlement westward into Iowa and Minnesota.

In 1832 fewer than fifty whites lived in Iowa; twenty years later, settlers had arrived in considerable numbers. Occupation had been rapid and steady. Briefly part of the Wisconsin Territory, Iowa became its own territory on July 4, 1838. Eight and a half years later, with a white population of more than eighty thousand, statehood followed. Settlement occurred mostly in the eastern part of the state along the Mississippi River; however, in preparation for further expansion, counties had been organized in western regions still controlled by American Indians. Six years after becoming a state, Iowa had two hundred thousand citizens.[6]

The typical white male settler moving to Iowa was twenty-eight to thirty-five years old, married, with children. He was a Protestant, Democrat, and farmer. His view on race relations was simple: do not allow blacks to live in the state and drive out all American Indians.[7]

These settlers partly got their wish when the federal government removed the Sac and Fox. On October 11, 1842, the Sac and Fox signed a treaty selling all of their traditional lands west of the Mississippi River for lands farther west. The treaty allowed the Sac and Fox to continue to live in Iowa for three more years, until 1846. However, instead of northern Iowa now being vacated of American Indians as whites wanted, various bands of Wahpekutes, pleased with the removal of their enemy, migrated into the area. They settled to the west of the Des Moines River. Among these new residents were Sintominiduta and Inkpaduta.[8]

Whites may have seen the newly opened northern Iowa region as theirs, but the Dakotas believed they still had claims to the area and were not pleased to find whites moving onto their lands. They were especially upset that among the incoming whites were a number of lawless frontiersmen. Henry Lott, typi-

cal of these border criminals, belonged to a gang of horse thieves
working around Fort Des Moines. In 1845, after the leader of the
gang was caught, Lott moved to Red Rock in Marion County.
Here he stole horses from American Indians, sold bad whiskey to
the Sac and Fox, and was so troublesome that local whites forced
him to leave the community. The following year, Lott moved
north to Pea's Point in Boone County. From his base here he
stole horses in Missouri and sold them in Wisconsin. Later in
1846, he moved to the mouth of the Boone River in Webster
County.[9]

Initially, Sintominiduta traded with Lott until he caught him
stealing half a dozen of his horses. In the winter of 1848, Sintominiduta and some of his men went to Lott's cabin, intending
to chase him out of the area. Lott and his stepson saw the approaching Dakotas and fled the cabin, leaving behind Lott's wife
and younger children. This included Milton, his twelve-year-old
son. Sintominiduta shot Lott's horses and cattle and smashed his
beehives. He told Lott's wife they had five days to leave the homestead. Milton, hoping to find his father, left the cabin but soon
became disoriented and died of exposure near Boonesboro.[10]

After leaving his family to an unknown fate with the vengeful
Dakotas, Lott went to Pea's Point, where he recruited the help of
Chemusa, called Johnnie Green by local whites, a leader of a
group of renegade Potawatomis. Chemusa and his men returned
with Lott to his cabin where the rest of Lott's family, except
Milton, was found terrified but unharmed. Discovering a barrel
of whiskey missed by Sintominiduta, Lott gave it to the Potawatomis in gratitude for their help before returning to Pea's
Point with his family. Never fully recovering from the raid and the
death of her son, Lott's wife died soon after. Lott swore revenge
on Sintominiduta and tried to claim three thousand dollars'
worth of damages from the federal government, but he failed to
obtain any compensation.[11]

It is not known if Inkpaduta accompanied Sintominiduta on

his raid against Lott, but it is clear that Inkpaduta agreed the lands of the Dakotas in Iowa must be protected, not only from certain renegade whites attempting to settle in northern Iowa but also from the government surveyors sent to map out the region. In 1848 James Marsh was hired to do a survey of public lands north of the Raccoon River. More specifically, he was to run a correction line from a point on the Mississippi River near Dubuque to a point on the Missouri River.[12]

Marsh's work took him to the Des Moines River near present-day Fort Dodge. Crossing to the west bank of the river, he advanced only one to three miles before running into Sintominiduta's band. Sintominiduta took a hard line with Marsh, ordering him out of the area. Even though his party was not armed, Marsh refused to leave and prepared to continue traveling westward, which Sintominiduta had no intention of allowing. Marsh was moving close to the Spirit Lake region of northern Iowa, an area of lakes and streams that fed into the Little Sioux River and the west fork of the Des Moines River. Spirit Lake and the Little Sioux valley had once been the home of the Mdewakantons before warfare with the Omahas and Iowas forced them into southern Minnesota. Even so, it was a favorite place of the Dakotas, and they still claimed ownership.[13]

When Marsh's refusal to leave threatened this important region, Sintominiduta reacted violently. He and his men destroyed Marsh's wagons and equipment and stole his provisions and horses. Unable to continue, Marsh returned to Dubuque, where he reported the incident.[14]

The following year, 1849, after driving off another surveyor party, Sintominiduta decided to strike against the settler homesteads on the Des Moines River near the mouth of the Boone River. It is likely that Inkpaduta participated in this destruction of cabins, robbery, and general harassment of the whites living along the Des Moines.[15] If Sintominiduta, or as the settlers now called him, "Old Head Devil," believed these actions would force the whites out, he was mistaken. Instead, the federal government sent the army to protect the settlers.

Fort Des Moines had been established in eastern Iowa in 1843 but closed three years later when the frontier moved farther to the west. In 1850 Maj. Samuel Woods and two officers and sixty-six enlisted men of Company E, Sixth Infantry, arrived at the mouth of the Lizard Fork on the Des Moines River. Here Woods constructed a fort for the protection of northwestern Iowa. Initially named Fort Clarke after the commander of the Sixth Infantry, Newman Clarke, the fort was renamed Fort Dodge in June 1851. This change was to honor two U.S. senators from Wisconsin and Iowa.[16]

The garrison was made up of well-seasoned troops. Company E had fought against the Seminoles in Florida and in the Mexican-American War. Typical of the time, 75 percent of the enlisted men in the company were either Irish or German immigrants. Major Woods, who had been in charge of the removal of the Sac and Fox from Iowa, knew the area well. The fort itself was roomy with more than enough space for the garrison, their wives and children, and a number of civilian employees. The post consisted of twenty-one buildings, including a steam-powered sawmill.[17]

At first the soldiers had little contact with American Indians. The Dakotas tended to stay away from the new fort, and not until June 1851 did the garrison meet them for the first time. The army was there not only to keep the peace between the Dakotas and the settlers but also to round up stray bands of Sac and Fox and Potawatomis that either had never left the area after the removal of their tribes or had returned.[18]

Iowa was not the only area where the Dakotas were feeling the pressure of white encroachment. The Lakotas on the plains were finding their expansion blocked by incoming settlers. The incoming whites used the overland routes across the plains and soldiers soon established military posts along these routes. In

1851 at Fort Laramie, the Lakotas signed their first treaty with the U.S. government granting whites the right to use the Overland Trail through their territory in return for annuity payments and goods. That same year, the Dakotas in Minnesota made an even more critical tribal treaty.

Similar to Iowa, Minnesota was experiencing a rapid increase in white settlement. When Minnesota was established as a territory in 1849, a census showed a white population of 3,814 civilians; between 1850 and 1857 the population increased fortyfold to 150,000 white settlers.[19] The demand for farmable land was intense, and the government took measures to obtain the land of the Dakotas and Ojibwas.

In the 1840s the Dakotas had been willing to sign the Doty Treaty to give up their lands in exchange for financial support, and conditions had not improved over the next decade. The game on Dakota lands was almost gone, and there was little left to hunt or trap in order to trade with the white traders. The traders had extended credit at high rates of interest; consequently, the Dakotas were deeply in debt from purchasing food and goods to survive.[20] With ever-increasing numbers of whites arriving in Minnesota, it was only a matter of time before the Dakotas were overwhelmed by them. Signing a new treaty seemed like the only option left to a desperate people.

In July 1851 negotiations with the upper bands of the Sissetons and Wahpetons were held at Traverse des Sioux, and with the lower bands of the Mdewakantons and Wahpekutes at Mendota, Minnesota. The Dakotas were not united on the issue of selling most of their lands in return for a reservation and annuity payments. Discussions and debates over the treaties were held among the bands and villages. The Wahpekutes favored signing the treaty, as they were almost destitute and in need of the supplies and food that the federal government promised.[21]

After several weeks, all four bands signed the treaties presented to them. The Dakotas gave up all rights to their lands in

Minnesota, Iowa, and present-day South Dakota — east of the Big
Sioux River and along a line from Lake Kampeska to Lake Traverse and the Sioux Woods River; this constituted some 24 million total acres of land. In return, the Dakotas were to receive a
payment of $275,000 up-front and another $1.4 million in annuities over the next fifty years. They were also to receive a reservation 150 miles long and 10 miles wide, located along both sides
of the Minnesota River. However, once money was deducted to
pay the massive debt owed to the traders and further money
removed for mixed-bloods, who were also to receive a payment as
members of the tribe, the Dakotas received only seven cents an
acre for the lands they sold. In June 1852 the United States
Senate ratified the treaties and the lives of the Dakotas changed
forever.[22]

Red Legs, another son of Tasagi, and Gray Back were two of
the Wahpekute chiefs who signed the treaty for their people.
Absent from signing the treaties were Inkpaduta and Sintominiduta. Neither man was invited to the treaty conferences nor were
they recognized by the government as band leaders. When Wamdisapa moved his village to South Dakota, Inkpaduta ceased to
have close connections with the other Wahpekutes. By the time
of the treaty conferences, Inkpaduta was not seen as a Wahpekute by the government officials at Mendota, nor did he live on
the lands ceded by the Wahpekutes.[23]

Given his resistance to white settlement in Iowa, it is not likely
that Inkpaduta would have signed a treaty giving up the Wahpekutes' land. It appears he was determined to retain control
over the Little Sioux River valley and make it his home. In fact, he
met with the Omahas, enemies of the Dakotas who also claimed
the valley region, to promote better relations and gain hunting
privileges extending to the Missouri River.[24]

Either way — by not being invited to the treaty conferences or
by refusing to accept the treaties — Inkpaduta and Sintominiduta were now seen as renegades by the federal government.

While the Dakotas began to move onto the new reservation, Ink-paduta continued to reside in South Dakota and Iowa with no intention of living on the reservation. Soon, because of poor conditions on the reservation, other Dakotas would leave it to wander over their traditional homelands.

In July 1853 Indian agent Robert G. Murphy began to survey and lay out the new reservation. There would be two agencies: the Upper Sioux Agency for the Wahpetons and Sissetons, and the Lower Sioux Agency for the Mdewakantons and Wahpe-kutes. By late summer the Dakotas began to move with much reluctance to the agencies. The Mdewakantons and Wahpekutes arrived in October. The Dakotas hesitated to settle on the reser-vation because of the lack of work completed at the agencies and the minimal amount of land plowed for crops. But hunger and the encouragement of annuities brought most Dakotas to the reservation by the end of November.[25]

Settling onto the reservation, the Dakotas found their econ-omy, culture, and society still threatened by the changes brought by the whites. Indian agents often failed in their duties, the traders' loose credit practices resulted in new debts, missionaries preached a new religion, and food was still lacking. The diet of the Dakotas changed from wild game to pork, beef, flour, and bread. Unable to sustain themselves by hunting, the Dakotas traded their annuity money for food from the traders, who charged high prices. Annuity payments in 1853 and 1854 were late in arriving. Without money to buy food, many Dakotas there-fore left the reservation to try to hunt and fish.[26]

What they found off the reservation were lands quickly being occupied by white settlers. Towns and villages were springing up in the lands ceded by the Sioux. In 1855 the editor of the *St. Peter Courier* proudly wrote, "Our prairies are settling up rapidly; set-tlement is extending up to the line of the Sioux Reservation, and now the traveler as he journeys onward, towards the upper agen-cies, is scarcely out of sight of comfortable dwellings, where but a few months since no claims had been taken, and nothing could be seen to break the monotony of the prairie scene."[27]

For other Dakotas, the answer to their problems was to embrace assimilation and accept the white approach to life. In 1856 some Dakotas — most having converted to Christianity and adopted white people's clothing — formed the Hazelwood Republic and embraced the practice of farming for their livelihood. To do this, they had to overcome traditional sex roles, with men now doing the farming. They also had to overcome a reluctance to use a plow rather than a hoe. The plow cut into the earth, in violation of their traditional religious beliefs. The Hazelwood Republic was controversial among the Dakotas and caused great friction with those who disapproved of the changes. Those who accepted assimilation were soon nicknamed "farmer" Indians by local whites, and those who clung to the traditional culture were labeled "blanket" Indians.[28]

Adding to the problems on the reservation was the mounting tension between the Dakotas and incoming settlers. Two cultures now strived to economically, socially, and culturally inhabit the Minnesota River valley. Quite often their views on hospitality, landownership, and race clashed, causing difficulties for both groups.

Friction started soon after the treaties of 1851. Dakotas claimed that German settlers near New Ulm, Minnesota, were occupying their lands and wanted them removed. The same issue emerged around Mankato, Minnesota. Complaints increased as more settlers arrived in the valley. Whites reported Dakotas entering their homes without warning, disrupting attempts to farm the land, and stealing food and livestock. The most common settler complaint, however, was the Dakotas' begging for food and goods. Often settlers were afraid or annoyed by the presence of wandering Dakotas.[29]

The Dakota practices of dropping by unannounced and begging illustrate a basic cultural misunderstanding. Since stopping by a neighbor's home unannounced was not considered rude or unacceptable behavior to the Dakotas, they did not understand the whites' objections. Furthermore, to the Dakotas, there was a difference between begging for food and goods and making a request for them. When the whites first arrived, the Dakotas offered them ducks, prairie chickens, and other game, along with maple sugar and wild rice. In this way they showed generosity and hospitality, both important virtues to the Dakotas. When whites were reluctant to share or refused to give food or gifts in return, the Dakotas saw them as stingy and socially rude, especially when the Dakotas were hungry and greatly in need.[30]

The Dakotas had complaints of their own. Whites showed little regard for the boundaries of the reservation, and some tried to settle and farm on lands belonging to the Dakotas. Other whites illegally sold alcohol to the Dakotas or stole their horses.[31]

In Iowa, relations between the settlers and those Dakotas who declined to live on the reservation were no better than in Minnesota. There were numerous small bands of Dakotas still living and traveling throughout northwestern Iowa. Many of them were Sissetons led by Red Thunder. Others were the remnants of the Red Top band, which had divided into at least four groups led by Sintominiduta, Inkpaduta, Titonka (Big Buffalo), and Umpashotah (Smokey Day).[32] Inkpaduta was no longer a subchief under Sintominiduta but a chief in his own right, although his village was small. He still respected Sintominiduta, and there was no falling out between the two men, who often traveled and hunted together.

Most of the roaming Dakota bands lived along the Des Moines River from the forks up to the Spirit Lake region and along the Little Sioux River at Buffalo Grove, Twin Lakes, or the headwaters of the Boone River.[33] They had their share of confrontations with white settlers in the area. The Dakotas harassed white settlers, told trappers and surveyors to leave, and stole horses and other

items. Governor James W. Grimes of Iowa took the problem
seriously, calling upon the federal government to send military
troops to the area; however, the incidents were fairly minor.[34]

In 1851, however, two more serious incidents occurred. Five
white families who were originally from New England lived along
the Boyer River, sixty miles southwest of Fort Dodge. While most
of the settlers were working in the fields, a group of thirty to forty
Dakotas raided their cabins; stole food, goods, and horses; and
kidnapped a young married couple from one of the cabins.
When the raid and kidnappings were discovered, some of the
farmers followed the culprits but could not catch them. Messengers were sent to Fort Dodge. Lieutenant Lewis Armistead,
who later gained fame for his part in Pickett's Charge at the
Battle of Gettysburg, led thirty soldiers and six civilians in pursuit of the kidnappers. The raiding party fled north toward Spirit
Lake, covering their trail as they went. The members of the raiding party finally scattered into smaller groups, which hindered
tracking by the pursuers.[35]

Armistead proceeded up the North Lizard Creek, where he
came upon Umpashotah's small village comprising only five or
six lodges and thirty to forty people. Although he found no
evidence in the village of the raids or of the missing white couple, Armistead arrested Umpashotah and continued his march.
At Granger Point, near present-day Estherville, Iowa, the path of
the raiders broke up into many trails, most heading toward the
Des Moines River. By this point Armistead and his men had been
on the chase for ten days; the soldiers were tired and the weather
was turning cold. Advancing to the Des Moines River, they came
upon Inkpaduta's village. They searched his camp but found
no stolen items or evidence of the kidnapped pair. Frustrated,
Armistead arrested Inkpaduta and another man, Chaskanah.
Along with Umpashotah, all three were taken back to Fort
Dodge and placed into the post stockade. They were to be held
until the white couple was returned.[36]

William Williams was the post sutler for Fort Dodge and was present when Inkpaduta was jailed. He described the subchief as being in his mid-fifties—obviously Inkpaduta looked much older than he was. He was approximately five feet, eleven inches, with stout broad shoulders, large head, broad, pockmarked face, sunken and black sparkling eyes, and a big mouth. Inkpaduta and the others were held for ten days before the Dakotas responsible for the raid came to the fort with the couple and some of the stolen goods. Inkpaduta was released and allowed to leave the fort.[37]

In an attempt to portray Inkpaduta as a savage, many writers often list the kidnapping of the white couple as one of his "sins." However, no evidence of the crime was found in his camp, while the kidnappers eventually came forth and returned their prisoners while Inkpaduta was in custody. Although it is likely that Inkpaduta had participated in the harassment of local settlers and surveyors in an effort to protect the Little Sioux River valley—a prime area for hunting and trapping—he more often than not had good relations with whites.

For example, Inkpaduta and his followers trapped along the Little Sioux River and traded furs with neighboring whites. Martin McLeod, a trader originally from Traverse des Sioux, Minnesota, knew Inkpaduta well and found him to be a good credit risk for up to fifty to sixty dollars, a decent amount of money for the period.[38]

Although he maintained good relations with local whites, Inkpaduta was surprised and at times angered by the meanness of some whites. Settlers would order him away from their farms or sic their dogs on him and his people. This reflected the cultural misunderstanding referred to earlier: whites' desire not to have the Dakotas just drop by or ask for food. To Inkpaduta, this behavior was mean-spirited and not neighborly.[39]

Still, Inkpaduta did have a number of positive dealings with traders and settlers, with his closest white friend probably being

Curtis Lamb. In 1851 Lamb was the first man to settle in Smithland, Iowa. Smithland was a small community on the Little Sioux
River roughly thirty miles southeast of Sioux City, Iowa. Lamb
farmed and traded at Smithland with local Dakotas, including
Inkpaduta. From 1851 through 1853, Inkpaduta's band would
arrive at Lamb's farm in the fall and spend the winter. Lamb lent
Inkpaduta traps and traded furs with the village. In return, Inkpaduta had women supply the Lamb family with firewood. When
Lamb obtained enough furs, he would transport them to Kanes-
ville (present-day Council Bluffs) to sell them. As these trips kept
him away from home for days, Lamb would ask Inkpaduta to
watch over his family. Inkpaduta took the responsibility seriously, even hunting game to give to Lamb's wife.[40]

One reason Inkpaduta appreciated Lamb was that he did not
trade in alcohol. Inkpaduta told Lamb he did not trust many
traders because of their practice of using alcohol to obtain terms
more favorable to themselves. Drunkenness led to a serious incident near Lamb's farm in the fall of 1852. Two Dakota bands,
Inkpaduta's and another led by Wassebobedo, were encamped
near Lamb's property. After a bout of heavy drinking, a brawl
broke out between the inebriated men of the two camps. In the
fight, Wassebobedo was wounded and an unnamed brother of
Inkpaduta's was killed. Lamb tended to Wassebobedo's wounds,
an act that drew Inkpaduta's ire. Inkpaduta and several other
men, in war paint, came to Lamb's door and accused the trader
of protecting and aiding their enemy. Later, Inkpaduta calmed
down and did not hold Lamb responsible for aiding his brother's
killers.[41]

The following fall, Inkpaduta came to Lamb requesting his
help. White men were again in the area attempting to sell alcohol to the Dakotas. Inkpaduta opposed this, believing it would
lead to more problems and possible violence. Inkpaduta asked
Lamb whether he should take matters into his own hands and
bust up the whiskey barrels and drive the traders out. Discerning

that this would not be the best course of action, Lamb advised Inkpaduta to wait. He went with Inkpaduta to speak with the traders, getting them to leave voluntarily.[42]

In the spring of 1856 Lamb and his family moved to Sioux City. He sold his farm to a Mr. Livermore. When Inkpaduta's band returned in the fall, they did not find their friend as expected. Livermore was unfriendly and not open to the Dakotas camping on his farm. Inkpaduta decided to winter near the Adams farm, another local white known and liked by the Dakotas.[43]

Although Inkpaduta wintered in Iowa, he did not spend all of his time there. He often journeyed into South Dakota and Minnesota. Inkpaduta frequently traveled with Sintominiduta. Sintominiduta liked to hunt along the Minnesota and Blue Earth Rivers and would often spend the winter along the Blue Earth near Mankato, Minnesota. Having good relations with whites, Sintominiduta even enrolled two of his children, a son named Joshpaduta and a daughter, in a Mankato school. Mrs. Sarah Marsh remembered the children to be around eleven and twelve years old, "extremely bright," and willing to teach the Sioux language to the other children as they themselves learned English.[44]

While whites in Minnesota liked, and were impressed by, Sintominiduta, once again Inkpaduta's physical appearance seemed to bring forth a negative reaction from settlers. A citizen of Mankato, who described Sintominiduta as a "magnificent specimen physically," referred to Inkpaduta as "not nearly as good looking a man" and called him "ugly," noting his smallpox scars.[45]

Not all interactions between the citizens of Mankato and Sintominiduta went smoothly. In the fall of 1853 Sintominiduta stored a crop of wild rice in the attic of Thomas D. Warren, a local trader. Sintominiduta proceeded to run up a debt of twenty-five dollars and then failed to pay the bill. Warren refused to return the rice to Sintominiduta until he covered the debt. An angry Sintominiduta later returned to Warren's house accompanied by armed men. Neighboring whites who saw the warriors armed themselves and came to Warren's defense. Fortunately, both Warren and Sintominiduta were willing to talk over their disagreement and eventually worked out the problem. Sintominiduta gave Warren a gun, and Warren returned Sintominiduta's rice, plus five dollars.[46]

Although they generally enjoyed good contacts with whites, Inkpaduta and Sintominiduta had not changed their view on retaining control of lands they believed belonged to the Dakotas, especially the hunting grounds in Iowa. It was the firmness of their position that led to new troubles for Inkpaduta and a tragic death for Sintominiduta, an incident that affected Inkpaduta's relationship with white settlers. The troubles commenced with the 1853 closing of Fort Dodge.

Under the terms of the treaties of 1851, all Dakotas were supposed to be living on the reservation along the Minnesota River in Minnesota. To oversee this reservation, the army decided to build a new post, Fort Ridgely, rendering Fort Dodge obsolete. On April 18, 1853, Major Woods and most of the garrison started their "most difficult and toilsome" march overland to Fort Ridgely. Two months later, Lt. James Corley led the remaining troops out of the abandoned post.[47]

Fort Ridgely was located on the north bank of the Minnesota River roughly eighteen miles from the Lower Sioux Agency. The role of the post's garrison was to assist the Indian agent in distributing the annuities and keeping the peace on the reservation, interdict whites trying to trespass on the reservation, and act as referee between the Dakotas and white settlers. Not happy with conditions on the reservation or with the traders and Indian agents, the Dakotas often turned to the military for support. Army officers were usually critical both of living conditions on the reservation and of the Indian agents appointed by the government. They were convinced the army could do a better administrative job than the Indian Bureau.

The new post had a larger garrison than Fort Dodge, usually two to three companies of infantry or artillery. Several of the post buildings were made from local granite, while the rest were constructed with wood. A popular post, its main drawback was its location. Built on the high ground above the Minnesota River, it was surrounded by deep ravines on three sides. With no palisade, the fort was vulnerable to attacks from the ravines; but with the Dakotas safely on the reservation, it was deemed unlikely the fort would ever be assaulted. Less than a decade later, this assumption was proven wrong.

With the closing of Fort Dodge, relations between the Dakotas and whites in Iowa quickly worsened. Settlers were harassed and their livestock and other property stolen.[48] Still refusing to accept the treaties of 1851 or leave the Little Sioux River valley, Inkpaduta made peace with the Omahas to better protect this location. He became a willing participant in new incidents to intimidate incoming whites.

Although Inkpaduta was not responsible for the 1851 kidnapping of two local settlers, two years later, following the closing of Fort Dodge, he was most assuredly involved in a new kidnapping. In late fall 1853, Inkpaduta took prisoner two men, James Chambers and a Mr. Madden, who had been hunting along the headwaters of the Cedar River. Chambers convinced Inkpaduta that he and Madden were also traders who had left their wagon of goods some miles away. Inkpaduta sent four men with them to retrieve the wagon. After walking six miles, Chambers noticed a grove of trees and told the Dakotas that the wagon was located there along with other white men. Chambers convinced the men guarding them that he and Madden would go to the grove and tell the white men not to shoot, and then bring the wagon back out to the waiting Dakotas. The warriors fell for the ruse, and Chambers and Madden ran away once they disappeared into the grove.[49]

An aggravated Williams, the former sutler of Fort Dodge who

remained behind after the post closing, asked Inkpaduta to meet with him. After speaking with Williams, Inkpaduta agreed not to take any more whites prisoner.[50] Inkpaduta's capture of Chambers and Madden, while frightening for the two men, in the end harmed no one. It was more an act of harassment than of any evil intent. Overall, Inkpaduta was still interacting well with most whites during this period. This remained true until Henry Lott brutally murdered Sintominiduta and his family.

After being driven out of his home by Sintominiduta, Lott was forced to leave Iowa in 1851. Soon afterward, Lott and his step-son returned to Iowa. In the autumn of 1853, after earlier being chased off the Fort Dodge military reserve by soldiers, the two men settled in Humbolt County at the mouth of what came to be called Lott's Creek, near the upper Des Moines River. They brought with them three barrels of whiskey for trade with American Indians.[51]

In January 1854, having never forgotten Sintominiduta and wanting revenge, Lott learned the chief and his family were en-camped twenty-five miles north of Fort Dodge. Sintominiduta had recently returned from Minnesota to winter in Iowa. Lott went to the chief and asked him if he wanted to join him and his son on an elk hunt. Perhaps he did not recognize or remember Lott, as Sintominiduta readily agreed. While hunting, Lott shot and killed Sintominiduta. Returning to Sintominiduta's camp, Lott and his son proceeded to murder the chief's aged mother, two wives, and two of his four children. His son Joshpaduta was wounded but survived, while a daughter hid herself and was unharmed. Lott dumped the bodies into a small nearby stream and tried to make the massacre look like a band of renegade Sac and Fox had attacked the family. Afterward, Lott and his son sold Sintominiduta's possessions and furs to settlers on the Boone River and fled the state.[52]

Inkpaduta and his band were on Lizard Creek when the mur-ders took place. Two weeks later, Inkpaduta found the bodies.

He took them to the nearby town of Homer, seeking justice from civilian authorities. Knowing that the Dakotas were greatly upset about the murder of Sintominiduta and his family, Williams came from Fort Dodge to see Inkpaduta. He found Inkpaduta's camp nine miles from the former post up the Des Moines River, with its members in mourning. Williams and L. Ketzman, an ex-soldier from Fort Dodge, offered to try to find Lott. Four of Inkpaduta's men went with them but could not pick up the trail of the fleeing culprits.[53]

A Polk County grand jury indicted Lott for murder, and a coroner's jury was held in Homer to review the case against him. John Johns, the city coroner, and Granville Berkeley, the prosecuting attorney, made a mockery of the investigation. Sintominiduta's head was brought before the jury; his surviving daughter and his son Joshpaduta testified to what they had witnessed of the massacre, and other Dakotas, including Inkpaduta, were questioned. Inkpaduta and the other Dakotas kept repeating in Sioux, "White men kill Dakota, kill Sintominiduta." Berkeley claimed the Sioux language had its roots in the Greek language and proceeded to "translate" what the Dakotas were saying. In the end, the whole hearing was turned into a farce, and nothing resulted from the grand jury investigation.[54]

Inkpaduta had been promised the white authorities would take the murder investigation seriously. He and the other Dakotas were angry when Berkeley made a mockery of Sintominiduta's death. Berkeley infuriated the Dakotas further when he took Sintominiduta's head and nailed it to a pole outside his house, where it remained for the viewing of any curious whites passing his home.[55]

Having failed with the civilian authorities, Inkpaduta turned to the military for assistance. Traveling to Fort Ridgely, he met with the commandant, Major Woods. Woods promised to look into the case and sent out a patrol, which proved unable to locate Lott and his son. Sintominiduta's murder was no small event to the Dakotas. Even on the reservation, there were hard feelings over the murders, and Woods felt compelled to call several Dakota leaders to the fort to discuss the matter. Woods assured them that Lott would be apprehended and warned the assembled leaders to not cause any trouble or he would "blow them to hell." Woods also informed Superintendent Willis Gorman of the murder of some Sioux "not included in the treaties of 1851" but expressed confidence the Dakotas on the reservation would not retaliate.[56]

Whether the attempts by the white authorities, both civilian and military, were in earnest or halfhearted, Lott was never arrested for Sintominiduta's death. It is unclear what became of him after the killings; it is rumored he was either hanged by vigilantes in California or killed while trying to rob an emigrant wagon train somewhere in the West.[57]

In their early-twentieth-century state history, *Minnesota in Three Centuries*, Lucius Hubbard and Return Holcombe attempted to blacken Inkpaduta's reputation over his reaction to Sintominiduta's death. "It is doubtful whether Inkpaduta ever heard the particulars of All Over Red's [Sintominiduta's] death," they wrote, adding: "It is certain that he would not have been concerned if he had. With him it was every man for himself; he never had a sentiment so noble and dignified as that of revenge, and would not turn his heel to retaliate for the slaughter of his nearest friend." They concluded by asserting, "Of all the base characters among his fellow outlaws, his nature seems to have been the vilest, and his heart the blackest."[58]

It has been argued by many authors that Sintominiduta's murder led Inkpaduta to commit a revenge raid on the settlers at Spirit Lake. Obviously Hubbard and Holcombe disagreed with this theory, believing that Inkpaduta was so vile he would kill simply for pleasure. Evidence contradicts their opinion.

Following the murders and the failure to find Lott, many settlers commented about a change in Inkpaduta. He was outraged at the lack of justice and the seemingly cavalier attitude of the whites to the murders. He was furious over the beheading of Sintominiduta and Berkeley's sideshow display of the skull. Whites grew afraid of him and his constant talk about Sintominiduta's murder. One settler remembered Inkpaduta often talking of revenge for the killing. There is even a rumor that Inkpaduta started to drink after the incident.[59]

None of this means the death of Sintominiduta caused the Spirit Lake massacre. Samuel Pond, a missionary to the Dakotas, noted that they "were not remarkable for retentive memories . . . If they did not avenge an injury soon after it was inflicted, it commonly went unavenged."[60] The murder of Sintominiduta occurred nearly three years before the Spirit Lake Massacre, and it is unlikely to have been a direct cause of Inkpaduta's attack on the settlers. However, the ever-growing numbers of whites, many of whom were unfriendly and afraid of the Dakotas, living on what he believed were Dakota lands, coupled with the increased difficulty of feeding his people and of continuing to live a free nomadic life, the murder of Sintominiduta surely added to the resentment Inkpaduta felt with the invading settlers.

Following the death of Sintominiduta, Inkpaduta was never as friendly toward whites as he once was. Although he had committed some minor crimes against whites prior to the murder, his harassment against the settlers became more serious and frequent. The next few years laid the groundwork for the Spirit Lake massacre.

## CHAPTER 4

# *"A Fearful Mistake"*

## SMITHLAND AND THE SPIRIT LAKE MASSACRE

After being falsely accused of regicide, fratricide, and kidnapping, Inkpaduta soon committed an act of brutal violence, the massacre at Spirit Lake, so heinous to whites he would never outlive his actions — not just for the remainder of his life, but also in historical memory. Because of the brutal murders of the settlers around the Okoboji Lakes as well as at Springfield, Minnesota, settlers, writers, and historians made the case that Inkpaduta was an inveterate hater of all whites — a man of utter evil.

Following the attacks in 1857 on the isolated settlers of northern Iowa and southern Minnesota, new judgments were leveled against Inkpaduta. Abbie Gardner, whose family was slaughtered in the massacre, understandably saw Inkpaduta as "a savage monster in human form, fitted for the darkest corner of Hades." In the 1930s Minnesota historian Frank Herriot compared Inkpaduta to Milton's Satan. He claimed that Inkpaduta's hatred of whites was "intense, relentless and notorious," adding, "Historians have given Inkpaduta an unenviable reputation for sheer brutality, ruthless ferocity and abominable treachery." Herriot concluded that historians were right in their evaluation. In his history of Iowa, Benjamin Gue also condemned Inkpaduta but blamed his evil partly on his being an American Indian; his band was made up of "cowardly savages" who took advantage of the isolation of the settlers "with the relentless cruelty of his race." An "Indian gangster" was how historian Edgar Stewart referred to Inkpaduta.[1] To understand the massacre that would change Inkpaduta's life forever, one must understand the circumstances affecting Inkpaduta and the Sioux by the mid-1850s.

By the 1850s the entire great Sioux nation that spread from Montana and Wyoming in the west to Minnesota in the east was under pressure from white encroachment. In 1851 the Dakotas sold all their lands in Minnesota and Iowa and moved onto a reservation with a bleak future. In 1858 they would sell all their reservation lands, on the north bank of the Minnesota River consisting of 1 million acres, while farther west, the Yanktons and Yanktonais sold part of their territory to the federal government.

The Lakotas signed the 1851 Fort Laramie Treaty, which did not involve the sale of any land but which, in return for annuity payments, allowed whites to pass peacefully through their region on roads protected by the U.S. Army. This treaty was intended to keep the peace, but failed. In 1854 the first war between the Sioux and the incoming Americans occurred over the killing of a cow.

In the summer of that year, several thousand Lakotas gathered around Fort Laramie awaiting the promised annuities. While they waited, an emigrant train of Mormons heading for Utah passed by the village of Conquering Bear, a Brule chieftain. A cow broke loose and ran into the camp. It was killed by a hungry Miniconjou visitor to the village named High Fore Head. The owner of the cow complained to the army at Fort Laramie. Foreseeing trouble over the incident, Conquering Bear went to the fort to pay for the cow. Unfortunately, two young inexperienced officers commanded the small garrison of Company G, Sixth

Infantry. They refused to accept payment and demanded the arrest of High Fore Head.

The next day, Lt. John Grattan, a recent graduate of West Point, led twenty-eight soldiers, two artillery pieces, and a drunken interpreter to Conquering Bear's village. He insisted High Fore Head be handed over to him. Conquering Bear tried to explain that he could not turn over a visitor to his village and again offered to pay for the cow. After a useless discussion, the soldiers opened fire. The artillery was situated too high, and the volley did little damage to the Sioux, except mortally wounding Conquering Bear. Surrounded by more than one thousand armed and ready Lakota warriors, Grattan and his entire command were quickly wiped out.

Reacting to the so-called Grattan Massacre, the administration of President Franklin Pierce and the army demanded war. In 1855 Gen. William Harney led an expedition of both cavalry and infantry into Lakota territory and attacked the camp of Little Thunder. The surprise assault caused heavy losses among the villagers, including women and children. Shocked by the ruthlessness of the attack and not wanting a war in the first place, the Lakotas quickly met with Harney and sued for peace. By 1856 the First Sioux War was over; however, the Lakotas never forgot the humiliation of their quick defeat.[2]

In 1855, unsure what effect the war would have on the Dakotas living on the reservation in Minnesota, the Commissioner of Indian Affairs ordered that no money or firearms were to be supplied to the Dakotas until Maj. Hannibal Day, commander at Fort Ridgely, confirmed the Indians were not planning any reprisals in support of their western brethren. Viewing the measure as an overreaction by the Indian Bureau, Day quickly judged conditions on the reservation to be peaceful, and the annuity payment was made.[3]

The Dakotas were not intending war, but pressures were

mounting on those living on the reservation and those still nomadic. Minnesota's white population was increasing to the point the territory would soon be a state. Towns and farms surrounded the reservation, making any form of hunting very difficult.

Survival was also an issue for those Dakotas still living in Iowa. White population growth there was even more rapid. By the mid-1850s three railroad lines had reached the Mississippi River, making movement into Iowa quite easy. The first settlers established themselves mainly along the Mississippi River, but the summer of 1855 saw a new surge of settlement into northwestern Iowa. Whites staked out land claims along the Little Sioux and Des Moines Rivers up into southern Minnesota. The tree-lined streams and fertile soil made the region very attractive to land-hungry farmers. Isolated farms and communities began to appear all over the area, including the main town of Smithland. By December 1856 even the Spirit Lakes region — an area important to the Dakotas — had thirty-nine settlers living on widely scattered farm sites. In the 1860 federal census, the state of Iowa had a white population of 674,913.[4] For nomadic bands such as Inkpaduta's, this massive influx of settlers made their ability to continue to hunt and provide for themselves a critical issue.

For Inkpaduta, now middle-aged, the traditional life he knew growing up as a Wahpekute had changed dramatically. The yearly cycle of spring trapping and the planting of crops, a summer of hunting and gathering, the fall harvest and deer hunt and then a quiet winter, was long over for most of his people. Forced onto the reservation in Minnesota, the Santee were close to starving and divided into factions either favoring or rejecting assimilation. The assimilation efforts of the Indian agents, reservation officials, and missionaries were causing great tumult to the social and cultural values of the Dakotas. Refusing to live on the reservation, Inkpaduta resisted these changes as he and his band tried to hang on to the traditional life of his people. Born among a free, independent people, Inkpaduta was now one of the last holdouts against the rising tide of white encroachment.

Following the death of Sintominiduta, Inkpaduta and his band spent the summer of 1854 in Dickinson County, Iowa, around the region's lakes. He also camped near Dakota City, later renamed Humboldt, and at Glen Farm. Over the next few years, Inkpaduta journeyed from the Missouri River northward to the Cheyenne River and to the upper Des Moines River to the south and east. Normally roaming over southwestern Minnesota and northwestern Iowa, Inkpaduta also spent time in what is now South Dakota. He would often camp on the lakes around present-day Madison, South Dakota, and along the James River with the Yanktons, with whom he shared kinship bonds. But he mainly liked the Little Sioux valley region of Iowa, where he would live in the fall and winter hunting elk and deer and fishing and occasionally fighting traditional Dakota enemies.[5]

In July 1854 Inkpaduta took part in a revenge raid against the Ho-Chunks. Three or four Ho-Chunks had killed a Sioux, and the Dakotas responded with an attack on the Ho-Chunk reservation. Local settlers became involved when Inkpaduta and some men searched two homes for possible hidden Ho-Chunks. A militia was formed to force the Dakotas to leave the area. Tensions increased when a Mr. Dickerson, a farmer, struck a warrior for breaking his grindstone. Goods and money were, at first, offered to the angry Dakotas, but with the arrival of reinforcements from Mason City, the whites demanded back the goods and money and insisted the Dakotas leave the area.[6]

Soon afterward, Inkpaduta went to the Dakota reservation and tried to obtain an annuity payment. The Indian agent refused him, most likely because Inkpaduta had not signed the treaty in 1851 and was not seen by whites as a Wahpekute.[7]

There is no doubt that Inkpaduta's relationship with whites had gone sour. The murder of Sintominiduta followed by the pathetic grand jury investigation, bullying by armed militias, and finally, the refusal of an annuity payment compounded his growing anger and frustration with local settlers. In 1855 Inkpaduta struck back on numerous occasions.

He began to strip trappers of their traps and harass surveyors. In the spring near Dakota City, Iowa, he plundered the cabin of E. McNight before encamping around Spirit Lake with other Dakota leaders including Umpashotah. In July, at Kossuth, Iowa, he and his men robbed cabins until settlers threatened violent retaliation, causing Inkpaduta to return the stolen items and leave. The next month, Inkpaduta arrived at the cabins of Ambrose Call and another man named Maxwell. At first, everything went well; but soon the Dakotas entered the cabins and robbed the men. Call and Maxwell confronted the Dakotas and ordered them to depart. Maxwell's wife went for help and returned with several armed farmers. Call, who remembered Inkpaduta as "a large middle age" man, insisted that he leave the area. Inkpaduta replied that his men were out hunting elk and that after returning they would depart the next day. They did so in the morning.[8]

After a tense summer in Iowa, Inkpaduta moved north to the Dakota reservation to once again attempt to obtain annuity payments. This time he was successful. He received annuities for himself and eleven of his men. Inkpaduta briefly remained on the reservation before returning to spend the winter in Iowa.[9]

The winter seemed to have a calming effect on Inkpaduta, and 1856 was as peaceful as the preceding year was strained. The spring found Inkpaduta and his band living on the upper branches of the Little Sioux River. From that location they crossed over to the headwaters of the Des Moines River. Inkpaduta no doubt was in good spirits because the hunting was excellent, ensuring his people had sufficient food and provisions.

After spending the summer near Algona, Iowa, Inkpaduta decided to again ask for a share of the annual annuity payment.

The agent was reluctant to pay, stating that Inkpaduta was not recognized under the treaties of 1851. Other Dakotas, some assuredly his kinsmen, spoke up for Inkpaduta, explaining that his blood ties and marriage ties to the Wahpekutes and Sissetons entitled him to the payment. An Indian Bureau official, Kintzing Prichette, reported that the Wahpekutes had backed Inkpaduta's claim only because they feared revenge if they did not. This conjecture has been commonly accepted ever since. However, this explanation was not likely the case as Inkpaduta had good kinship ties with the Wahpekute band as well as the Sissetons; in addition, he had never harmed anyone inside the tribe. Yet, perhaps some Dakotas were beginning to believe the rumors of Inkpaduta as many whites already did.[10]

The agent agreed to furnish annuities to Inkpaduta. Inkpaduta also requested annuities for the eleven men of his band. While on the reservation awaiting the payment, one of his sons, Roaring Cloud, married a Wahpekute woman. Following the payment, Inkpaduta headed west to present-day South Dakota before again returning to Iowa.[11]

Along the way Inkpaduta camped near the small community of Springfield, Minnesota, near the Iowa border. There he found forty-two settlers and William Wood, a local trader. The Dakotas camped near the town and traded on credit, with Inkpaduta promising to return in the spring to pay Wood. Relations were good, with Inkpaduta's people boasting to the settlers that they had never harmed a white man.[12]

By the fall of 1856 the makeup of Inkpaduta's band was fairly well established. Charles Flandrau, the Indian agent for the Dakota reservation, estimated the band consisted of eight to ten lodges. The annuity payments made in 1855 and 1856 list Inkpaduta and eleven other adult males. This record places the village population at probably fifty to sixty people.[13]

Inkpaduta's immediate family dominated the band. He had two wives, at least five sons, two daughters, and one grandchild in the camp. Three of his sons, the twins Roaring Cloud and Fire Cloud and seventeen-year-old Big Face, were grown men. Two younger sons, probably Inkpaduta's second set of twins, Sounds The Ground As He Walks and Tracking White Earth, were also mentioned on the annuity lists. Roaring Cloud and Fire Cloud were both married; Roaring Cloud was married for only a few months, but Fire Cloud may have had children by this time. Both of Inkpaduta's daughters were married to men in the village, Rattling and His Old Man. The two men were Yanktons, thus providing Inkpaduta kinship ties to that band.[14]

Of the final six men in Inkpaduta's band at least one, a Sisseton named Shifting Wind, was married; however, it is likely others were married as well. His Mysterious Feather, also known as Sacred Plume or Sacred Feather, was approximately sixty years of age. His Great Gun, Putting On As He Walks (or Putting On Walking), One Leg (or Red Leg), and One Who Makes Crooked Wind As He Walks constituted the remaining male members of the village.[15]

After visiting Springfield, the band camped at Loon Lake in Minnesota before crossing into Iowa for the fall and winter. The hunting was still good, allowing Inkpaduta and his men to feed the village with little problem. In November a small party of white men, O.C. Howe, R.V. Wheelock, and B.F. Parmenter, guided by a hunter named Wiltfong, discovered the Dakota camp on Loon Lake. After a peaceful visit, the white men continued on their way.[16]

Shortly after this encounter, Inkpaduta crossed the border into Iowa. He intended to winter along the Little Sioux River. As he and his people traveled, they often met with white settlers living in the area. The village camped near the home of the Wilcox brothers in Large Grove and later by the Weaver cabin. As they hunted, trapped, and fished, interaction with the whites was open and friendly. This positive relationship continued as Inkpaduta and his people passed through the towns of Peterson,

Cherokee, and Peary. Clearly, Inkpaduta's anger over what had happened to Sintominiduta had waned. There is no evidence he hated all whites or was plotting their destruction. While at Peterson, Roaring Cloud and Fire Cloud competed against the settlers in shooting and wrestling contests.[17]

Sadly, an event that neither the American Indians nor the whites could control ended this peaceful interlude. On December 1, 1856, the pleasant fall came to an abrupt end with a massive blizzard. For three days and nights, the storm raged throughout northern Iowa, dumping more than three feet of snow over the area. This storm was followed by new blizzards, one right after the other, until there were snowdrifts of twelve to twenty feet and temperatures of thirty-seven degrees below zero. It remained cold throughout the spring, with some snow drifts remaining until July.[18]

As food supplies ran low, the isolated snowbound settlers feared they would not survive the winter. Jane Bicknell, a young girl living in Peterson, remembered one farmer coming to her parents' cabin to ask for food. He had been living on nothing but potatoes for three weeks. After getting some supplies, he later returned with his wife; they were completely out of food. The Bicknells let the couple stay until January 3, when, afraid they would also run out of food, Mr. Bicknell told the couple they had to leave. The forlorn farmer later froze to death; the fate of his wife is unknown.[19]

Unable to hunt in the deep snow, Inkpaduta's people ate whatever they could, living off muskrat, skunk, and finally their own horses. They frequently requested food from the settlers in Peterson, and the whites often gave what they could. The Dakotas always showed their appreciation for the much needed aid. Leaving Peterson and heading south, Inkpaduta and his band passed by other communities and farms, paying for food and other goods as they went. Even in the midst of a brutal winter, in which, as one settler remembered, "human endurance and human patience were strained to the breaking point," the Dakotas and whites continued to support one another until Inkpaduta's band reached Smithland.[20]

On December 9, 1856, Inkpaduta's band reached the outskirts of Smithland. They erected nine lodges, near the farm of Elijah Adams on the Little Sioux River, two miles from the town. Elijah and Rebecca Adams and their four children — Elizabeth, Wallace, Henry, and three-year-old G.E. — had arrived in Smithland the previous June. Originally from Kentucky, the family had moved to Indiana and then Illinois before coming to Iowa. At Smithland, Adams built a sturdy cabin measuring 16' × 32' × 12' and having a "partition across the middle and a good room upstairs." Inkpaduta's village remained near the farm for the next two months, and relations between the settlers and the Dakotas were initially peaceful.[21]

Soon after their arrival, Inkpaduta and several of his men came to the Adams cabin, where they sat and smoked a peace pipe. "We got right well acquainted with them as there was some of them in our house almost every day," Wallace Adams remarked. He added, "The Indians were quiet and sociable all winter." The Dakotas and their neighbors shared the same waterhole, while the women of the village visited with Mrs. Adams and her daughter, trading beadwork and other crafts for clothes and food. Other whites traded corn and pork for venison and moccasins. When cattle started dying from the cold winter, the Dakotas would take some of the meat from the dead animal to eat. Yet, Wallace Adams recalled, they never touched a live cow, even though the Dakotas were very hungry and in dire need.[22]

Other settlers echoed similar positive opinions. James McDonald remembered that "the Indians were friendly, always begging for food." "Everyday some of the Sioux Indians visited our cabin on a begging expedition," stated Mary Hawthorn Bouslaugh. She also noted the extremely hard winter and the fact that the Dakotas suffered greatly from hunger and the cold.[23]

Adams, one of the last white men to spend any time with Inkpaduta, recalled the appearance of the chief and his sons. He
remembered Inkpaduta as being around 160 to 170 pounds,
with light-colored skin and powerful arms and legs. His hands
were long and strong, and he spoke with a low, deep voice. He
had a "gruff and sullen" face, walked slowly, and was showing his
age, which Adams placed at sixty, although Inkpaduta was likely
in his early forties. Inkpaduta wore blankets with leggings fas-
tened to his belt, a blouse, and a cape pulled over his head.[24]

Adams believed Roaring Cloud and Fire Cloud to be approximately twenty to twenty-two years of age and referred to them
as "two big coarse chaps." By contrast, he remembered the
younger Big Face as being "tall and handsome" but also surly,
sullen, and possessing a bad temper.[25]

While at Smithland, Inkpaduta and his men went out to hunt
elk trapped by the large snowdrifts. They ate the meat and
traded the skins with the settlers for corn. When the settlers'
supplies began to run low, Inkpaduta and another man left their
village with elk and deer skins to trade with the Omahas for corn.
Successful, Inkpaduta returned later that winter.[26] By that time,
relations with the whites had turned bitter.

As the winter conditions worsened and food sources dwin-
dled, the citizens of Smithland had begun to resent the presence
of Inkpaduta's band. They were a drain on the remaining supplies. A series of incidents brought this resentment to the fore.

In the fields below Smithland, women from Inkpaduta's camp
dug out unhusked corn left by the farmers after the fall harvest.
Gathering it together, they proceeded to carry it through Smithland to their camp. Seeing the much-needed food they themselves had left in the fields, whites now accused the American
Indian women of stealing the corn. They whipped them with
switches and forcefully took it away from them. In another incident Dakota men were trailing a wounded deer they had shot,
only to have a white man claim it was as his. In another hunting

incident, a settler's dog attacked a group of Dakotas hunting elk. One of the Indians shot and killed the animal. Furious over the killing of his dog, the settler attacked the man responsible, beating him and taking away his gun. Finally, some young men from Smithland, probably intoxicated and intent on rape, attacked several Dakota women at a stream, chasing them back to their village. In retaliation for these acts, the Dakotas began to shoot cattle belonging to the farmers.[27]

The citizens of Smithland held a meeting at which they accused the Dakotas of stealing corn and hay and of generally being undesirable. A militia was organized to drive the Dakotas away from the community. Elijah Adams and his sons were not informed of the plan. Another settler, D.T. Hawthorn, refused to join the militia, believing the attitudes of the settlers were unjust and that there was no reason to turn on the Dakotas. Seth Smith was made the captain of the eighteen- to twenty-one-man militia. A militia major back in Ohio, Smith had kept the uniform and wore it now to take command. "That magnificent suit of regimentals" was how one recruit referred to it. In early February 1857—with his cocked hat, gilded epaulettes, split-tailed coat, and glittering sword raised high—Smith led his men to Inkpaduta's village.[28]

The militia took Inkpaduta by surprise. Four of his men were out hunting, but the rest of the people were in the village as the whites arrived. Speaking through a mixed-blood interpreter named Charley, Smith told Inkpaduta the militia wanted Inkpaduta to leave the area but only after the Dakotas first turned over all of their guns. Inkpaduta was stunned by this demand. Without guns for hunting, his people would not survive the winter; it was a death sentence. He promised Smith he would leave and stated there was no reason for the militia to take their guns. He appealed to the settler's fairness and sense of justice. Adamant, Smith responded that the Dakotas were indeed leaving and the whites were going to keep their guns. Pleading with Smith, Inkpaduta tried to explain that with the harsh winter and without guns, they all would starve—including women, children, and babies. Smith coldly told him to go to the Omahas. Without guns, Inkpaduta replied, the Omahas would kill them. Advancing into the village, the militiamen ripped the camp apart and seized all the guns they found. The women ran into the woods as Inkpaduta and his men looked on helplessly. Having finished their mission, the militiamen returned to Smithland, taking the guns with them. That night, Inkpaduta and his people departed.[29]

In his 1930s study of the Sioux, historian Doane Robinson wrote that Inkpaduta's people had been "insolent and quarrelsome" while encamped at Smithland. He blamed all the problems that transpired there upon Inkpaduta's people, claiming the Dakotas had been stealing and threatening the whites to the point that the brave men of Smithland had to disarm the troublemakers.[30] This statement hardly fits the facts and the testimony of settlers living in Smithland, who place the bitter winter and the whites' fears as the real causes for the march of the militia to expel Inkpaduta. The events at Smithland ended forever any peaceful coexistence between Inkpaduta and white Americans.

Inkpaduta left Smithland an angry man. Cultural and social differences had always divided the Dakotas and whites. Compounding these tensions was Inkpaduta's desire to retain control over the Little Sioux River valley and maintain his independence. Then came the murder of Sintominiduta. Rather than avenge the murder, Inkpaduta had instead turned to the civilian and military authorities for justice—and was let down. Finally, as his people fought to survive the winter of 1856–57, whites stripped them of the only means they had of securing enough food. Heartlessly, Smith made it clear that the whites could care less if Inkpaduta and his band lived or died. This point was driven home to Inkpaduta in a very personal way shortly after he was forced out of Smithland as his grandchild died from exposure and starvation. All of these events pushed Inkpaduta over the edge. He gave in to his anger, an emotion his relatives said could, at times, consume him and make him resort to irrational actions. "The People made a fearful mistake," Adams commented when Smithland drove out the Dakotas, adding, "for this was the direct cause for the Spirit Lake Massacre." Descendants of Inkpaduta and other Dakotas today agree that Inkpaduta was forced by the actions of the whites into committing the attack at Spirit Lake. It was a simple matter of survival. Ambrose Little Ghost, the great-grandson of Inkpaduta, believes hunger drove Inkpaduta to fight in an effort to survive.[31] Inkpaduta was only weeks away from committing the massacre that would make his name infamous.

Before leaving Smithland, the Dakotas made two stops. Inkpaduta first went to the cabin of Elijah Adams. There he traded four buffalo robes for a light double-barreled shotgun. Adams did not yet know of the militia's move against the Dakotas and innocently swapped a gun for the robes. From the Adams farm, Inkpaduta went to the home of David Hawthorn, the Adamses' nearest neighbor. Hawthorn was not there, but his wife and four small children were in the cabin. Inkpaduta and his men entered the house and proceeded to sharpen their knives and axes while making threatening gestures to the children. Mrs. Hawthorn sent one of the children to the Adams farm to get help. Adams quickly arrived and after giving the Dakotas some ammunition and blankets, got them to leave the cabin in peace.[32]

After departing Smithland, Inkpaduta's band headed north toward Spirit Lake. On February 20, 1857, the four hunters rejoined the camp, along with the two guns they had taken with them. The band had also retrieved several of their guns from a farmer named Livermore, who had been part of the militia and had kept four of the confiscated guns. After Inkpaduta paid Livermore five dollars and discussed at length the band's intention of leaving Smithland, the farmer returned the guns.[33]

Angry and bitter, Inkpaduta, prior to the return of the hunt-

ers, had worked his way up the Little Sioux River stealing and
looting. The Dakotas stole food and weapons from settlers,
shot cattle and other livestock, and entered cabins where they
smashed furniture and ripped up clothes and blankets. On February 15 they reached Peterson, where just weeks before they
had spent pleasant days interacting with the settlers. This time
they ransacked homes and kidnapped three women: a Mrs. Taylor, Mrs. Harriett, and Harriett Mead. On February 17 at the
Taylor home, warriors beat Mrs. Taylor's husband and kicked
her son into the fireplace where he suffered serious burns, before taking Mrs. Taylor away along with Mrs. Harriett. The next
day, they forcibly took Harriet Mead, a younger girl, from her
father's cabin. Inkpaduta's men carried the women back to their
village and raped them before setting them free.[34]

Departing Peterson, Inkpaduta's men also struck the homes
of Mr. and Mrs. Weaver and Almer Bell, which were a few miles
outside of the town. At Bell's farm they shot cattle and looted the
cabin. Totally rearmed, the band continued to move northward
along the river.[35]

Twelve miles to the north of Peterson was the small community of Gillett Grove. Once again, the Dakotas looted cabins and
raped two more women. A settler named Gillett fought back.
When a warrior started to harass his wife, Gillett shot the man
dead. Gillett then fled with his family and brother to Fort Dodge.
It is not clear which member of Inkpaduta's band was killed, but
his death did put the village in the mood for a revenge raid.[36]

The Gilletts were not the only ones fleeing to Fort Dodge for
safety. Word had already reached that community about the new
outbreak of violence. William Williams collected a militia of
some fifty men and followed Inkpaduta's trail to the town of
Cherokee before turning back. He saw the trail heading for
Spirit Lake and, not realizing any whites lived there, believed the
Dakotas could do no further damage. The militia returned to
Fort Dodge.[37]

Although often referred to as Spirit Lake, the lake region of
northwestern Iowa actually consisted of three large and several
smaller lakes. The three largest were West Okoboji, East Okoboji, and Spirit Lake. *Mini-Wakan* in Sioux means "Spirit Water,"
and this was the name given to the area. It was a scenic area with
beautiful lakes surrounded by woods of cottonwood, basswood,
and oak trees. By the summer of 1855 whites had explored the
lakes but had not settled in the area. It was not until July 1856
that the first settlers arrived.[38]

Rowland Gardner and his wife, Frances, were from Seneca,
New York, where Rowland had worked in a comb factory. A strict
Methodist who abstained from drink or smoking, the thirty-
seven-year-old Rowland had moved with his wife and their four
children — Mary, Eliza, Abigail, and Rowland Jr. — to Ohio in
1852. Still not satisfied, the Gardners later moved to Indiana and
then to Iowa. Along the way, the Rowlands' oldest daughter,
Mary, married Harvey Luce. They and their two children followed the Gardners to the frontier.[39]

Gardner built a 15' × 20' cabin with a loft on the south shore
of West Okoboji Lake. As the Luces' cabin was not yet completed, they lived with the Gardners. Within eight months, several more families and a number of single men joined the growing, but widely spread out, community. James and Mary Mattock
and their five children were the Gardners' closest neighbors on
West Okoboji Lake, roughly one mile away. Robert Madison and
his fifteen-year-old son, John, lived with them.[40]

On East Okoboji Lake, William and Carl Granger shared a
cabin with two other men, Bertell Synder and Dr. Isaac Harriott.
The twenty-six-year-old Harriott enjoyed the rough life on the
frontier. In a positive happy tone, he wrote friends about the
cold, the lack of provisions, the isolation. Farther up the east
shore of the lake lived Joel and Millie Howe with their six children, who ranged in age from nine to twenty-three. The Howes'
oldest daughter, Lydia, was married to Alvin Noble, and the No-

The Gardner cabin, the only remaining cabin of the Spirit Lake massacre. Photograph by Evans. Courtesy of the Minnesota Historical Society.

bles and their son, Jonathan, lived close to the Howes. The last cabin on East Okoboji Lake belonged to Joseph and Elizabeth Thatcher, four miles from the Gardners' residence [41]

Only one family lived on Spirit Lake itself, the largest of the three main lakes: William and Margaret Marble's cabin was the most remote home along the lakes. Though located miles from their nearest neighbors, the religious Margaret would hold worship services and invite the other settlers to attend. There were also several bachelor shanties, and single men traveling through the area often stayed at the cabins of the various families. By the winter of 1857 some forty people lived along the lakes.[42]

The people at Spirit Lake were living on the very edge of white settlement. Only Springfield, Minnesota, eighteen miles to the north, was more remote. Spirit Lake was one hundred miles from Fort Dodge and forty miles from Gillett Grove. The nearest telegraph office was in Dunleith, Illinois. By March 1857 the long, cold winter isolated the settlers even further.

On March 7 Inkpaduta and his band reached the lakes, setting up camp less than a mile from the Gardner cabin. The whites knew nothing of the events at Smithland or subsequent recent events. A letter written by one of the settlers dated March 7, 1857, mentioned the arrival of Inkpaduta's band but expressed no fear and mentioned trading with them. That night, sounds of a dance could be heard coming from the Dakotas' village.[43] It was probably a war dance as the band prepared for a revenge raid, a type of warfare in which everyone — women and children included — were fair targets.

On the morning of March 8, Rowland Gardner woke up earlier than usual in preparation for a journey to Fort Dodge for supplies. It was a beautiful day, with temperatures in the forties and the sun shining; it was the first real springlike day. Similar to other communities, the settlement at Spirit Lake was running short of provisions. Harvey Luce, Joseph Thatcher, and several other men had previously left with some oxen to purchase supplies. On the return trip, fighting their way through the snowdrifts, the men and animals had stopped for a needed rest. On his own, Luce had pushed on, reaching Spirit Lake on March 6. At this point, Gardner had decided to obtain further provisions.[44]

Gardner and his family were busily preparing for his departure when Inkpaduta and the men of his camp appeared outside the cabin. One man wanted food, and Frances gave him some. Then another man demanded food. Before long, all of the Dakota men were in the cabin eating. When the food ran out, Inkpaduta demanded ammunition. The situation grew tense as one of Inkpaduta's sons pointed a gun at Harvey Luce, who grabbed the barrel and forced it away from his body. The Dakotas then exited the house, shooting several of Gardner's cattle as they left.[45]

Soon after, at 9:00 A.M., Dr. Harriott and Bertell Synder came to the cabin with letters for Gardner to take to Fort Dodge. Gardner informed them of the hostile actions of Inkpaduta and of his decision, given what had happened, not to go to Fort Dodge that morning. Harriott and Synder returned to their cabin, only to learn that the Dakotas had harassed the Mattocks; James Mattock was now asking for their assistance. Harriott, Synder, and Joe Harshman, a visitor staying at the Granger cabin, armed themselves and went to help the Mattock family. Carl Granger remained behind to protect his house from any roving Indians.[46]

At noon Inkpaduta's men ran off the rest of Gardner's and Luce's cattle. Concerned for their neighbors, Luce and Robert Clarke, a visitor lodging with the Gardners, left at 2:00 P.M. to warn the Mattocks and the men at the Granger cabin. Roughly an hour later, shots were heard from the direction of the Granger cabin. Unknown to the Gardners, Luce and Clarke had been ambushed and killed. Gardner did not know what to think after hearing the shots. Unsure if he and the others should stay in the cabin, Gardner was afraid to leave the presumed safety of the house. Hoping that Luce and Clarke would return, Gardner decided he and his family should flee to the Mattock cabin, a bigger and more defensible building.[47]

Before they could leave, Gardner noticed nine warriors approaching the cabin. He quickly barred the front door and prepared to fight. Fearing what would happen if her husband, the only man in the house, tried to fight so many, Frances Gardner pleaded with Rowland to unlock the door and let them enter. Fatally, Rowland did what his wife requested. The Dakotas came in and demanded more supplies. As Rowland turned to find them some food, he was shot in the back. Frances and Mary Luce were pinned down, beaten to death, and then scalped. Thirteen-year-old Abbie Gardner held her brother Rowland Jr., age six, and her two cousins, four-year-old Albert and one-year-old Amanda, close to her as her parents and older sister were murdered. Then, as the children screamed and cried in terror, the warriors pulled them from her, one by one, and either beat them to death outside the cabin with pieces of firewood or picked them up by their heels and then slammed them headfirst into the posts of the door. Abbie was not killed, but was abducted.[48]

Unknown to Abbie, her family members were not the only ones to die that day. Prior to the slaughter at the Gardner cabin, Harriott, Synder, and Harshman had reached the Mattocks' homestead. It was decided that James and Mary Mattock and their children would return with the men to the Granger cabin. Somewhere along the route back to the Grangers', they were ambushed; all were killed. It appears the men put up a fight, with Dr. Harriott wounding one of the attackers. But caught out in the open, the settlers had no chance. Behind them, the Mattocks' cabin was set afire. Back at his farm, Carl Granger also was killed, standing in the doorway of his home.[49]

By the end of the first day of the massacre, nineteen people were dead; Abbie Gardner was taken prisoner. Brought back to the Dakota camp, Abbie watched that night as the villagers cele-

Postcard depiction of Abbie Gardner's capture by Inkpaduta's band. Courtesy of the Minnesota Historical Society.

brated their victory and performed a scalp dance. As they danced, Abbie saw Inkpaduta, whom she described as "a savage monster in human form, fitted only for the darkest corner of hell."[50] The killings would resume in the morning.

The next day, eight warriors left the village. Their faces painted with black charcoal—black being one of the traditional war colors of the Dakotas—they headed up the east shore of East Okoboji Lake toward the Howe and Thatcher cabins. Before reaching the first cabin, the group encountered Joel Howe walking toward the Granger homestead; he was planning to obtain some flour. They brutally killed Howe, subsequently cutting off his head and throwing it into the lake. Continuing on to the Howe cabin the war party found Millie, Joel's wife, and their six children. The Dakotas rushed the building, killing everyone they found. Mrs. Howe quickly hid under a bed while her children died around her. In their hurry, the warriors did not plunder the cabin but moved on to the Thatcher farm. Joseph Thatcher was away getting supplies, but his wife, Elizabeth, and their small three-week-old baby girl, Dora, were there, along with Alvin and Lydia (Howe) Noble and their two-year-old son, Jonathan, and Enoch Ryan.[51]

When the Dakotas first arrived, they acted friendly, but soon they made demands and insulted Elizabeth Thatcher and Lydia Noble. As matters started to intensify, Alvin Thatcher and Enoch Ryan both tried to resist but were shot dead. The Dakotas ripped Dora Thatcher and Jonathan Noble from their mothers' arms, carried them outside, and then bashed the infants by their heels into an oak tree until they died. Elizabeth and Lydia were taken prisoner.[52]

After plundering the cabin and shooting the livestock, the war party returned to the Howe cabin to loot it. Here they discovered Millie still hiding under the bed and killed her. Lydia Noble, mourning the loss of her family, noticed that her brother, thirteen-year-old Jacob, was still alive; he was badly beaten and propped up against a tree. She urged him to crawl into the house and hide. Jacob tried but a warrior soon spied and shot him.[53] The war party took the two captive women to Inkpaduta's camp, where they found Abbie Gardner and discovered the fate of their neighbors. The Dakotas abused and later raped the women.[54] Twelve more people died on the second day of the massacre.

On March 10 Inkpaduta used horses and sleighs to move the Dakota village across the iced-over West Okoboji Lake. The sleighs were laden with food and other loot taken from the settlers. The following day, the village encamped in a grove north of the Marble homestead on the southwest shore of Spirit Lake. From here Inkpaduta sent out scouts to determine whether there were any other whites in the area. They discovered the Marble cabin on March 12, but the Dakotas stayed in their camp that day, feasting on stolen food. Not until the next day, March 13, did the massacre resume.[55]

As at the Thatcher cabin, the Dakotas approached the Marble home acting as friends. They asked for food, which Margaret Marble provided, then invited William Marble to join them in a shooting contest. After William fired his weapon, he walked toward the target. He was shot in the back and killed. Seeing her husband fall, Margaret ran for the woods but was immediately captured and taken back to the village to join the other three women.[56]

By that time the killings at Spirit Lake had ended — thirty-two people were dead. Traveling slowly, with the sleighs weighed down with supplies and goods, Inkpaduta and his band left the area and headed north into Minnesota toward the village of Springfield. The raid was not over yet.

## CHAPTER 5

# "A Perfect Panic"

## THE AFTERMATH OF SPIRIT LAKE

Within days, news of the massacre spread across much of the Midwest. Settlers in Minnesota, Iowa, and western Wisconsin feared for their lives, believing that hordes of Sioux were preparing to slaughter them at any moment. This hysteria caused thousands to flee from their farms and smaller communities for the safety of larger towns or makeshift forts. Innocent Dakotas were attacked in their camps or arrested on sight. Not even the future events of the Dakota War of 1862 caused the level of panic that the rumors and false stories of Inkpaduta's raids instigated.

A military expedition from Fort Ridgely and two civilian militia groups from Iowa attempted to apprehend Inkpaduta; all of them failed. The inability to capture Inkpaduta only added to his mystique and his image as a savage bent on resisting all things white. Writers added new villainy to Inkpaduta's infamy. Based on his supposed knowledge of Inkpaduta, Indian agent Charles Flandrau was among the first after the massacre to write about Inkpaduta. Flandrau proclaimed Inkpaduta as "one of the best haters of whites in the whole Sioux nation." In the first book on the massacre, L.P. Lee agreed with Flandrau, adding that Inkpaduta was "universally reputed as one the most blood-thirsty Indian leaders in the northwest."[1]

When the Dakota War erupted just five years after the massacre, a new accusation was added to the sins of this great enemy of the whites: Inkpaduta was one of the main individuals behind the uprising. As early as 1908, author Edward Curtis blamed Inkpaduta along with Little Crow for being the main instigators of the war. Curtis called him bloodthirsty, fiendish, but a "capable leader." More recently, Michael Clodfelter and Maxwell Van Nuys have continued to champion this view of Inkpaduta. Clodfelter maintained that Inkpaduta and his men were heavily involved in the war, stating they were at the Battles of Wood Lake and Fort Abercrombie and certainly behind many of the deaths caused during the conflict. Inkpaduta was "deliberately, vigorously, and bloodily to oppose peace" with the whites is how Van Nuys depicted him. To Van Nuys, Inkpaduta was the leader of the Sioux who promoted all-out war with the Americans and "eventually he was to pursue, and direct, this policy on a scale seldom exceeded in American Indian history."[2]

Awareness of the massacre at Spirit Lake came even before Inkpaduta left the area. Morris Markham, a local trapper, had lost a pair of oxen. On March 6 Luce, returning from his trip to obtain supplies, told Markham he had seen them near Big Island Grove. Markham set out to find the oxen and fortuitously missed the start of the massacre. Around 11:00 P.M., on March 9, Markham returned from his unsuccessful search and discovered the bodies at the Gardner cabin. Alarmed, Markham went to the Mattock, Granger, and Howe homesteads to warn them, but he only found more signs of the disaster. At one point he nearly wandered into Inkpaduta's camp but realizing the danger, he quickly fled. Crossing the frozen lake, Markham next found the victims in the Thatcher home. After spending the night sleeping in a ravine,

Markham headed to the nearby settlement at Granger's Point on the Des Moines River. He stopped at George Granger's cabin and told Granger about the massacre and death of his brother, Carl. After a short rest, Granger and Markham left to warn the community of Springfield, twenty miles away, arriving on March 11.[3]

Markham was not the only person to stumble upon the remains of the Spirit Lake community. Robert Wheelock, B.F. Parmenter, Cyrus Synder, and Orlando Howe, four land speculators from Newton, Iowa, were on their way to the Spirit Lake region at the time of the massacre. Howe had been there the previous year and intended to settle in the area with his family in the spring. The other three men were coming to look over the region. William Williams warned them at Fort Dodge not to continue their journey. He told them about the hard winter and the near starvation of many people, adding that no one had been farther than twelve miles from Fort Dodge since the fall. Undaunted, the men loaded a sleigh and hand sleds with provisions and set out for the lakes.[4]

On March 15, after a hard journey, the men reached Spirit Lake. They first approached the Howe cabin. Calling out, they were unsure why no one came out to greet them. Entering the house, they discovered Mrs. Howe with a crushed skull and the mutilated bodies of two of her sons, Alfred and Philetus. Wheelock and Howe proceeded to the Thatcher farm, where they discovered more bodies. Shocked and stunned by what they found, not knowing whether danger was still close by, the group could not decide what action to take. Soon, a blizzard struck. Unable to stay for long in the gruesome cabin, they departed for Fort Dodge even as the storm raged around them.[5]

Conditions worsened. Hit by snow and bitter cold, the men became exhausted from sickness and lack of sleep and suffered from snow blindness. They finally reached a settlement called "the colony," where they could rest. Joseph Thatcher was present in the village. For the first time Thatcher learned that his wife and perhaps all of his family were dead. Parmenter was too unfit to continue, but the other three men left for Fort Dodge to relay the news of the attack.[6]

Arriving on March 20, the three men went immediately to Williams. He heard their terrible tale and took them to a Methodist church service where they informed the minister of what had transpired. Williams then asked the male members of the congregation to stay behind and volunteer for the militia. Wheelock and another man went to Webster City to raise another company for the coming expedition. After three days of preparations, ninety-one men left for Spirit Lake with little food and only a motley collection of guns, blankets, clothes, and equipment on March 24.[7] Meanwhile, the citizens of Springfield had also sent for help.

That winter, Springfield consisted of six or seven families and the Wood brothers. George and William Wood had established the community the previous spring when they opened a trading post on the west bank of the Des Moines River. Settlers who were mainly from Iowa soon joined the brothers. The newcomers built homesteads on the east side of the river, spreading out over seven to eight miles. In all, fewer than forty-five white people lived in the area. This included Dr. E. Strong. With the aid of Eliza Gardner, the only member of the Gardner family, besides her sister Abbie, to survive the massacre, Dr. Strong was caring for Robert Smith who had lost his right leg, and John Henderson, who had lost both legs to frostbite during a blizzard. Close by the white community was Umpashotah's small Dakota village, comprising four families, encamped a mile from the Wood trading post on the west bank of the Des Moines River. Nine miles farther upstream was another trading post run by Joseph Coursalle; several more Dakota lodges resided near this post.[8]

On March 9 a Dakota man named Black Buffalo came to the Woods' trading post and told the traders of a massacre at Spirit Lake. While the Wood brothers did not believe the story, other settlers were alarmed enough to take up defensive positions in two cabins. Confirmation of the attack at Spirit Lake came when Markham and Granger arrived. At first there was a discussion about going to assist the people at Spirit Lake. But not knowing the circumstances, the settlers decided to remain on the defensive at Springfield. Joseph B. Cheffin and Henry Tretts agreed to go to Fort Ridgely for help. Markham and Jareb Palmer left for Spirit Lake to ascertain if the massacre was as severe as Markham initially perceived it.[9] Within days Markham and Palmer returned with eyewitness evidence that the massacre had occurred and that Springfield was in danger. All hoped that the army would arrive before Inkpaduta and his band appeared.

Twenty-nine-year-old Charles Flandrau, who had been the Indian agent for the Dakota reservation since August 1856, was the first white man to encounter Cheffin and Tretts when they reached the Lower Sioux Agency on March 18. Flandrau immediately left for Fort Ridgely to relay the news brought by the two exhausted men. He informed Col. Edmund Alexander, commander of the post, of the massacre and requested troops be sent to apprehend Inkpaduta and his band. Alexander readily agreed. On the morning of March 19, he ordered Capt. Barnard Bee, Lt. Alexander Murray, and the forty-eight men of Company D, Tenth U.S. Infantry, into the field. Just three hours after receiving the orders, the two officers, Company D, an interpreter named Philander Prescott, a mixed-blood scout Joseph La Framboise, and Flandrau left the fort for Spirit Lake some seventy miles away. Flandrau was not pleased with the hasty preparations of the expedition. He later wrote, "They were equipped in about [the] same manner as they would have been in campaigning in Florida," adding, "their only transportation being heavy wheeled army wagons drawn by six mules."[10]

At Springfield, the Woods remained in their trading post, still convinced there was no danger; twenty-seven people fortified the Thomas cabin, and a dozen more stayed at the Wheeler farm. They remained there for two weeks waiting for a possible attack. As time passed and the feared assault did not materialize, tensions eased and most people started to relax. Women and children went outside for fresh air, and men returned to their farm work. One woman, Mrs. Stewart, pregnant and miserable from the overcrowded conditions, convinced her husband they and their three children should return to their own cabin. He finally agreed. Everyone expected soldiers from Fort Ridgely would arrive shortly.[11] But the community was not as secure as they assumed.

Loaded down with supplies, loot, and horses, Inkpaduta's band moved slowly into Minnesota. They eventually set up camp in a grove on Heron Lake, roughly fifteen miles northeast of Springfield. From there, Inkpaduta sent two men on a scouting mission to ascertain conditions at Springfield. He wanted to learn whether the settlers there had heard of the earlier attack and were prepared, or whether the community was unaware of events and ripe for a further raid.[12]

On March 20 the Indian scouts went to the Wood trading post, where they purchased eighty dollars' worth of gunpowder, ammunition, lead, and other supplies. They paid in gold coins, taken from the Marble cabin. This payment should have raised some suspicions in the Wood brothers; however, the brothers still dismissed the idea of any danger. This was not true of Umpashotah, who entered the store as the two men were leaving. After himself trying to warn the Wood brothers, Black Buffalo arrived at Umpashotah's camp and told him the grim news. Concerned, Umpashotah went to the store, where he inquired about the massacre with the two scouts, who confirmed that the whites around the lakes were indeed dead and that another attack was planned for Springfield. Quietly, Umpashotah began moving his village from the Wood trading post to a new camp nine miles away at Joseph Coursalle's post. That night, William Wood came to see Umpashotah, surprised at the unexpected departure of his village. Umpashotah informed Wood of what the scouts had told him and warned that Inkpaduta's band was nearby.[13] Apparently unable to appreciate the warnings he was receiving, Wood returned to the trading post and did nothing with this information.

As civilian militia and regular army expeditions made their way to the massacre site, on March 26 Inkpaduta's men attacked Springfield. Abbie Gardner remembered twelve men preparing for war that morning, arming themselves and putting on paint before leaving the camp. Their first objective was the Thomas cabin.[14]

After a morning of chopping wood, the men at the Thomas homestead were inside eating lunch. At two o'clock, eight-year-old Willie Thomas was playing in the yard when he announced he could see Henry Tretts returning from Fort Ridgely. Looking outside, David Carver exclaimed, "Yes, it is Henry Tretts." Everyone rushed outside, eager for news. They were met with a volley of small-arms fire from the woods. It was not Tretts but a warrior dressed like a white man. Thomas was hit in the left arm; Carver was shot in the right arm, side, and lung; and Miss Drusilla Swanger was struck in the right shoulder as the people fled back into the cabin. Behind them lay Willie, groaning in pain from a shot to the head. He soon died on the doorstep of the house.[15]

Inkpaduta's men fired steadily at the cabin for over an hour but inflicted no further losses on the defenders. Inside the home, five men — Thomas, Carver, Jared Palmer, Morris Markham, and a man named Bradshaw, along with Louisa Church — returned fire as best they could.[16] The struggle became a stand-off.

Hearing gunfire, William Wood left the trading post and proceeded down to the river to investigate. As he crossed the stream, he was shot dead. His killers later dumped Wood's body in some bushes and set it on fire. Seeing his brother fall, George Wood ran for his life. He crossed the river and attempted to hide. The

INKPADUTA MASSACRE
MARCH 26. 1857 AN
OUTLAW SIOUX BAND UNDER
INKPADUTA MOVING NORTHWARD
FROM THE LAKE OKOBOJI
REGION OF IOWA WHERE IT HAD
MURDERED SOME THIRTY
PERSONS. ATTACKED THIS TOWN.
THEN CALLED SPRINGFIELD.
SEVEN SETTLERS WERE KILLED.
BUT A SPIRITED DEFENCE BEAT
OFF THE INDIANS AND SAVED
THE COMMUNITY.
A STATE MONUMENT
STANDS IN THIS PARK.

TWO BLOCKS EAST

Historical marker near Jackson (Springfield), Minnesota. Note that Inkpaduta's band is referred to as an "outlaw Sioux band." Courtesy of the Minnesota Historical Society.

raiders found and executed him, at close range. Warriors looted the trading post, taking ammunition to use in their attack on the Thomas cabin.[17]

Three warriors also approached the Stewart homestead. They acted friendly, calling out to Josiah Stewart that they wanted to trade gold coins for a hog. When Stewart went out to meet them, they shot and killed him. His wife, holding her newborn baby, and another child were also killed. Eight-year-old John Stewart hid behind a log and survived the murder of his family. He later went to the Thomas cabin for safety.[18]

The assault on the Thomas cabin continued until sunset. After driving off twelve head of cattle, the attackers withdrew. Meanwhile, Joseph Coursalle and three Dakotas from Sleepy Eye's band had encountered Inkpaduta's raiding party. Coursalle recognized Inkpaduta's sons, but later he did not mention whether Inkpaduta himself was among the attackers. Inkpaduta's men informed Coursalle of the murder of the Wood brothers and about the four women being held prisoner back in their camp. Coursalle then went to the Wood trading post and found the bodies of the two brothers.[19]

Rumors exist that other Dakotas joined in the attack on Springfield. Abbie Gardner claimed Inkpaduta met with certain Dakotas before the raid, and Thomas reported seeing Umpashotah, Sleepy Eye, and Joshpaduta (Sintominiduta's son) during the fighting.[20] With no other documented evidence, the truth of this assertion is doubtful. Umpashotah had tried to stay out of the way, even warning William Wood of a possible attack. Several men of Sleepy Eye's village were with Coursalle — not the attackers — and what happened to Joshpaduta after the death of his father is unknown.

With seven people dead and three more wounded, the badly shaken survivors of the attack decided to abandon the community and head for Fort Dodge. The settlers pulled out at midnight on sleds. In their haste, they left behind the two men crippled in the blizzard, Smith and Henderson, as well as a small baby belonging to A.P. Sheigley. The refugees struggled southward through the snow and encountered Williams's militia on March 30.[21] Williams then learned of this new attack.

Having left Fort Dodge on March 24, the expedition traveled only six to seven miles a day because of the rough winter conditions. The militia had been organized into three companies. Company A, under Captain Charles Richards, and Company B, commanded by Capt. John Duncombe, were from Fort Dodge. Company C was raised in Webster City, with Capt. John Johnson in charge. The advance toward Spirit Lake proved extremely difficult. Snow still lay deep over the land, and occasional storms left the men exhausted by nightfall. The glare of the sun off the snow and ice burned their hands and faces. Most difficult was maneuvering the supply wagons. Men had to march ahead and stomp down the snow to create a path for the wagons. Even with this advance work, the men had to rely on rope and their own muscle to pull the wagons and teams along.[22]

By the fourth day of the expedition, there was talk of turning back. With no wood for cook fires, the men existed on crackers and ham. After deciding to continue, the militia grew in strength to 125 men as farmers from the towns they passed through joined the column. Not until April 1 did Williams reach Granger's Point. Here he learned that Inkpaduta was long gone and out of reach of any punishment by the militia. Most of the men agreed to return to their homes, but Williams and twenty-five men went on to Spirit Lake.[23]

By the time it arrived at Spirit Lake the expedition had become a burial detail, finally laying to rest the victims around the Mattock cabin. Williams, mistakenly, believed the whites had put up a strong resistance there, leaving signs of hand-to-hand fighting. Williams estimated fifteen to twenty Indians were killed. The militia also found some forty to fifty dead cattle scattered around the site.[24]

Having tended to the dead, Captain Johnson and seventeen other men started out for Fort Dodge but were soon caught in a blizzard. Johnson and a private named Burkholder wandered off in the storm and froze to death. By the end of the expedition, another three men had died of pneumonia. In gratitude for the men's service, the State of Iowa granted a pension of twenty dollars to each surviving volunteer who served in the militia.[25]

The civilian militia were not the only ones suffering in the cold. Captain Bee, a forty-year-old career officer from South Carolina who would later die at the First Battle of Bull Run, remembered the army's effort against Inkpaduta in his report: "The narrative of a single day's march is a history of the whole. Wading through deep drifts; cutting through them with the spade and shovel; extricating mules and sleighs from sloughs, or dragging the latter up steep hills or over bare spaces of prairie." Bee left Fort Ridgely on March 19, after consulting with experienced guides about the most direct route to Spirit Lake. He and his men immediately encountered the terrible winter conditions. "The snow lay in heavy masses on the track which I was following," Bee wrote, "but these masses were thawing and could not bear the weight of the men, much less that of the heavy sleds with which I was compelled to travel."[26]

The army was forced to take a more indirect course — down the Minnesota River over to a trail leading through the village of Madelia on the Watonwan River, then overland to Spirit Lake. This route proved to be daunting for the soldiers. The men were freezing and soaked from the snow, mule teams got stuck in the snowdrifts, and all the while Flandrau criticized the army's effort. He claimed it was no better fit for a winter campaign than "an elephant for a ballroom."[27]

After a week of fighting through the snow, Bee's command reached the Slocum farm at the end of the trail. From there to the Des Moines River, it was "an unbroken waste of snow." While his men rested, Bee went in search of more supplies at South

Bend, a nearby community. In the meantime, Flandrau returned to the reservation. Bee continued his advance toward Springfield. Camping that evening on the Watonwan River, Bee felt compelled to train his tired men in skirmish tactics. Many of the soldiers were green recruits with little military training.[28]

On March 28, two days after the attack at Springfield, the soldiers arrived at Coursalle's trading post. Bee encountered some Sissetons and two mixed-bloods, Joseph La Framboise and Caboo. He learned about the raid from Coursalle. Coursalle believed that Inkpaduta was still in the area, staying in a nearby grove. That afternoon, at four o'clock, Bee surrounded the grove, only to find an abandoned campsite. Caboo raised Bee's hopes again when he said Inkpaduta was actually encamped fifteen miles away on Heron Lake. Led by Caboo, Bee, Lieutenant Murray, and twenty-three men mounted on horses and mules crossed the Des Moines River and marched to the lake. They found another deserted campsite. According to Caboo, the campfires were two to three days old. Bee concluded that Inkpaduta had evacuated the area and, given the winter conditions, could not be apprehended by his men. In fact, Inkpaduta was still on Heron Lake and was nearly discovered by the soldiers. When Bee's men approached the lake, Inkpaduta spotted them. Women doused the fire, pulled down lodges, and as they prepared to flee, assisted a wounded man who had been shot during the Springfield raid. The men prepared for battle, certain they would be attacked. Inkpaduta had moved his village the day before to some woods two miles from the old camp Bee had discovered. Bee sent men to search another lake close by but never looked in these woods.[29]

Having failed to find Inkpaduta, Bee sent Lieutenant Murray and twenty men to Spirit Lake to bury the victims of the massacre. With the rest of his command, Bee returned to Springfield, where he found the two injured men and baby and buried the seven people killed in the attack. On April 4 Bee set out for

Fort Ridgely; however, he left Murray and twenty-eight soldiers behind to reassure settlers that it was safe to return. Murray was relieved two weeks later by a twenty-man detail commanded by Lt. John McNab, who stayed in the area until the fall.[30]

The killing of thirty-nine settlers by a small band of roving Dakotas set off a panic never before seen in the Midwest. Settlers across Iowa, Minnesota, and western Wisconsin feared for their lives as stories of hundreds of warlike savages destroying town after town, murdering everyone in their path, rapidly spread over the region. Thousands of people fled their homes, while others built forts or organized militias for defense. The terror was more deeply felt because violence at the hands of the Dakota came as such a surprise. Other than the brief war with the Lakotas in the mid-1850s, there had not been any serious problems between the Sioux and the whites. Since the treaties signed in 1851, the Dakotas in Minnesota and Iowa had mainly resided on the reservation or at least stayed away from the majority of whites. Now a grim prospect faced whites on the frontier: if one band of Dakotas had struck violently, then perhaps all Sioux were preparing to fight.

The first reports of the massacre appeared on March 25 in the St. Paul newspaper the *Daily Pioneer and Democrat* and on April 2 in the *Des Moines Citizen*. The St. Paul paper placed the blame for the attack on a small band of Wahpekutes and stated the number of whites killed as fifteen. On March 26 the *Henderson* (Minnesota) *Democrat* also reported the attack, claiming seven to eight people died. The paper added that the story was probably false because the paper would have heard earlier if "trouble so extensive" with the Dakotas did exist. On April 16 the *Henderson Democrat* named Inkpaduta as the culprit responsible for the massacre. An editorial also spoke about the captured women "enduring the torments of a thousand deaths in every hour of their lives." Other papers called Inkpaduta an outlaw, hated by the Dakotas. In the view of the *St. Peter Courier*, "The murderers are outcasts, execrated by their own people, whose blood they desire." That the attack was executed by a handful of renegade Dakotas was soon lost in a wave of rumors and stories predicting a large-scale Indian uprising.[31]

Over the next two months, midwestern newspapers swept up in the mounting hysteria printed numerous reports of new Dakota offensives. The *St Paul Daily Times* reported that a band of Sioux had killed whites near Blue Earth and were marching on Mankato. Another paper stated that "savages" had advanced to within fourteen miles of Mankato, slaughtering every man, woman, and child in their path. Still other stories had Mankato and St. Peter destroyed by nine hundred Yanktons and Sissetons. "25,000 Indians in Arms!!" screamed one headline. In Iowa, Fort Dodge was reportedly under siege by five hundred to eight hundred Sioux warriors, and the *Oskaloosa Herald* claimed that fifty-three people were murdered on the Watonwan River.[32]

Such wild claims only intensified the feelings of vulnerability and imminent danger among area whites. Flandrau declared that an "intense panic" existed "all through the country." In Iowa, George Spencer wrote about his experiences in Boonsboro. The town was filled with refugees who all insisted that Fort Dodge and Webster City had been burned by Indians. "I never saw such a perfect panic or a greater pandemonium," Spencer remembered. In Kossuth County, settlers heard the flapping wings of sandhill cranes and mistook them for approaching warriors. Others believed visible prairie fires were the campfires of Dakota war parties. The *Fort Dodge Sentinel* claimed five thousand to seven thousand Sioux were moving down the Des Moines River valley. According to the *Keokuk Gate City*, the citizens of Fort Dodge had been massacred.[33]

In Minnesota, hundreds if not thousands of people fled their homes or small communities for the safety of larger towns. Cities including Mankato, New Ulm, St. Peter, Traverse des Sioux, and Henderson rapidly filled with terrified people who claimed they had seen their hayfields and homes burning behind them as they left. St. Peter contained up to fifteen hundred refugees, with no room to house more.[34]

Most people in southern Minnesota gave in to the panic gripping the region. There was a rumor that Fort Ridgely had been taken by the Dakotas. In Blue Earth City, citizens were roused from sleep at midnight by messengers warning of approaching hostiles. Half-clothed people ran desperately onto the prairie while others started to fortify a hotel. Journeying to Henderson for supplies, Thomas Scantlebury heard "a great excitement about the Indians, who have been murdering whites near Mankato." Soon after, a Dakota man and his wife entered Henderson to trade. They set off a panic causing whites to believe that three hundred Sioux were attacking. The couple was arrested. An eyewitness believed he had "never witnessed so much excitement — so many men bereft of common sense, and every trait that should characterize men on an occasion of danger." At Garden City, a new rumor of Indians raiding and burning sent people rushing to their newly finished fort. Many communities such as Judson, Nicollet, South Bend, and Eureka built stockades to defend themselves from attack. Traverse des Sioux placed women and children in fortified stone buildings.[35]

Yet, not everyone gave in to the surrounding fear. Edward Washburn, a settler living in Blue Earth County, wrote to his father about the hysteria he encountered. "I should not be much surprised if you have seen accounts something like this in the papers — The Indian War!! Terrible Slaughter! All Settlers on the Watonwan and Blue Earth Rivers have been Murdered and Scalped!" Washburn then wryly added, "We have just learned from authentic sources that every settler in Minnesota Territory, except one, has been murdered!" Washburn informed his father that the Dakotas were destitute and hungry and had been acting aggressively by taking food, plundering homes, and scaring settlers. He acknowledged the extent of the panic, noting, "Many of the settlers have left the country, and I have seen many women crying with swollen eyes, expecting that their infants and themselves would be scalped by the savages."[36]

Beyond the Midwest, news of the massacre and the supposed "Indian war" spread across the country. The *Chicago Democratic Press* reported that six hundred Sioux were raiding throughout Minnesota and had destroyed the city of Mankato. An account of the Spirit Lake massacre and the upheaval it caused was described in the *New York Daily Tribune*. James Denver, commissioner of Indian Affairs, received word from Francis Huebschmann, superintendent of Indian Affairs, that five hundred Sioux were invading the Des Moines River valley.[37]

With rumors of Indian offensives constantly repeated, some communities formed militia units to repel the supposed invaders. St. Peter raised three companies, commanded by the town's founder, William Dodd, to go to the aid of Mankato after a stagecoach driver, a Mr. Wagner, announced that fifty whites had died only twelve miles south of Mankato. Wagner claimed a force of five hundred to six hundred Yankton Sioux was moving on Mankato, committing atrocities on women; they "stripped them naked, took their scalps, and cut off their breasts." The citizens of St. Peter passed a resolution to go to the support of Mankato even as the Indians "advanced ten miles since the last report," burning everything behind them.[38]

On April 12 Dodd and the militia left St. Peter after requesting help from the soldiers stationed at Fort Snelling in St. Paul. News of the threat to Mankato caused the citizens of St. Paul to hold two town meetings. Two militia groups, the Pioneer Guards and Shield's Guard, hired a steamboat to take them upriver to Mankato and informed the army they were ready to offer support in the field. Colonel Smith, the commander at Fort Snelling, declined their aid. Instead, he ordered Capt. Frank Gardner and three companies—B, H, and E of the Tenth U.S. Infantry—to proceed to Mankato.[39]

Gardner reached Henderson on April 16 and Mankato two days later. Along the way he heard dire stories of St. Peter and Mankato lying in ruin and of nine hundred Sioux heading for St. Paul. He found these reports to be false. Once in Mankato, he spread his men out over the region to establish calm. Smith later summed up the expedition by stating there was "very large smoke, very little fire."[40]

The army had found no reason for alarm let alone an uprising to quell. Nonetheless, the militias still considered any American Indian to be hostile; one result of the Spirit Lake massacre was retaliatory violence toward and harassment of innocent Dakotas. One such group victimized by the harassment was the village of Red Iron. The five or six families of Red Iron's camp were Sissetons trapping and fishing on three small lakes while making sugar from maple trees in Watonwan County. Four German families became nervous over the presence of these Dakotas and banded together at the farm of Isaac Slocum. They also sent Joseph Cheffin to Mankato for assistance. On April 11, 1857, a thirty-eight-man militia commanded by Capt. William Lewis, a local doctor, hurriedly set off for the Slocum farm, arriving there that night.[41]

Coming upon the Dakota camp, the militia opened fire without warning. The Dakotas returned fire as they ran from the assault, retreating to a larger encampment on Sleepy Eye Lake. One villager had been seriously wounded and a militiaman had been struck by birdshot. Elated by their success, the white men started calling the affair the "battle of three lakes." Later, Dodd and his militia proceeded to Slocum's farm, having heard that the settlers and Lewis's men there were besieged by hundreds of warriors. Newspapers reported the skirmish claiming it was a fierce battle with twelve to fourteen Indians killed in the fighting. Meanwhile, hearing of another Sisseton village at the mouth of Perch Creek, Dodd and Lewis advanced there, only to find the camp deserted.[42]

Unfortunately for the Dakota band, who had made a timely escape from their Perch Creek camp, they ran into another thirty-man militia from Traverse des Sioux under Capt. George McLeod. The militia immediately started shooting, and the frightened Indians scattered. No one was hurt in the assault. Another militia, composed of Welch and German settlers under Col. S.D. Shaw, attacked the band and forced them to yet again run for their lives. Later, Shaw's men encountered the dead body of a German settler named Brandt. It is unknown who killed Brandt, but the Sissetons likely shot him in retaliation for the multiple attacks by the militias.[43]

The Dakota village of Sleepy Eye was another camp endangered by the hysteria stemming from the massacre. Warned by a company of home guards to move his people onto the reservation, Sleepy Eye left and set up camp on Swan Lake. In late April gunfire ripped through the village killing six men. Sleepy Eye fled to Fort Ridgely for protection.[44]

In fear for their lives, many Dakotas went to Fort Ridgely and requested the protection of the army. Some civilian whites also worked to protect the innocent American Indians. Thomas Cowan found Red Iron's band of eleven lodges and guided the members to a campground close to the post. Citizens of St. Peter later donated barrels of flour to Red Iron's hungry people.[45]

Although not mistreated, other Dakotas, like Umpashotah, were told to leave the area. Umpashotah had remained around Springfield following the massacre. On April 15 men from Algona, Iowa, surrounded his camp. They searched the five lodges of the village and found no loot or other evidence of involvement in the massacres. Released, Umpashotah moved to Spirit Lake, where he was confronted by Iowa home guards. Umpashotah agreed to leave the area forever, but two years later he returned to Spirit Lake — only to be arrested and ordered once more to depart the lakes region for good.[46]

It is ironic that the Dakotas turned to the army for assistance, receiving a generally positive response from the military while white civilians criticized the army for failing to apprehend Inkpaduta. Flandrau was an early critic of Bee's expedition. Williams, although his militia also failed to capture Inkpaduta, soon voiced criticism of the army's efforts. Williams claimed that Bee put too much faith in information obtained by Joseph Coursalle and the two mixed-blood scouts, La Framboise and Caboo. Caboo had told Bee that the campfires at Lake Heron were two days old when in fact Inkpaduta had left them only hours before. Williams implied that Coursalle, La Framboise, and Caboo all were secretly supporting Inkpaduta and wanted him to escape.[47]

Newspaper editors soon voiced their views against the army. The *Henderson Democrat* maintained that if there had been mounted troops stationed at Fort Ridgely, the murderers would have been taken. The editor demanded the army take to the field to find and punish Inkpaduta and called upon the military to kill the murderers immediately if taken. "If you don't punish them," he wrote, "within two years will be a general uprising by all the Indians." The editorial concluded: "Are they to go unwhipped of justice? Are our citizens to be butchered by the Indians with impunity? . . . For the honor of our country, for the future security of our settlements, for the sake of common humanity, we hope not." An editorial in the *St Peter Courier* echoing these sentiments stated, "It is highly important that these rascals should be promptly punished, unless we would give encouragement to other Indians that the most flagrant outrages may be committed against the frontier settlers with impunity." Two months later, an editorial in the *Henderson Democrat* criticized the army's inaction as the Sioux would see this as a sign of weakness. The editor relented somewhat by saying it was not the fault of the soldiers at Fort Ridgely but rather the War Department for placing only infantry at the fort and then too few of them.[48]

The *St. Peter Courier* agreed that mounted troops were needed and also blamed the incident on the lack of soldiers in general at

Fort Ridgely. However, the paper did not fault Bee; in fact, the *St. Peter Courier* supported Bee by publishing a letter from the officer that defended his expedition.[49]

If civilians were unhappy with the army's efforts to capture Inkpaduta, most officers were also frustrated with their inability to apprehend him. On a visit to St. Peter, Lieutenant Murray admitted the Bee expedition had been bungled. In his report to the Assistant Adjutant General, Colonel Alexander acknowledged that the winter conditions had caused Bee to fail. He called for a two-pronged offensive involving one hundred men from Forts Ridgely and Snelling to hunt down Inkpaduta when the warm weather returned.[50]

By May 1857 the hysteria had waned. In a brief column, the *Brownsville Southern Minnesota Herald*, admitted that stories such as the burning of Mankato had been exaggerated and that there had been no Indian uprising after all. An employee on the reservation, A. Robertson, wrote Flandrau of his regret in getting swept up in the panic. Still, the territorial legislature conducted a special session and passed three resolutions in response to the affair. The legislature requested that the military station dragoons at Fort Ridgely to be used to pursue Inkpaduta and asked the governor to place all the Dakotas on the reservation and make every effort to rescue the four captive women.[51] Besides their inability to capture Inkpaduta, the greatest concern for whites was the prisoners taken during the massacre. Whites continued to wonder what had happened to the women after their capture at Spirit Lake.

Forced to remain in the village during the attack on Springfield, Abbie Gardner remembered the twelve men who had participated in the raid returned to camp with twelve horses and much loot. One of them was wounded but still able to travel. After nearly being spotted by Bee and his men, Inkpaduta showed little haste in leaving the area. With more than a month's worth of captured supplies to sustain them, the band moved to the Pipestone quarries in southwestern Minnesota to wait out the worst of the winter weather. Inkpaduta and his people remained at the quarries for three to four days, making pipes before resuming their leisurely journey westward.[52]

At first, everyone rode on the horses or in the sleighs. But the sleighs broke down in the rough terrain and soon some of the women and all of the prisoners were forced to walk. The white women, who were forced to carry loads of up to seventy pounds, were kept apart from each other and verbally abused. Margaret Marble recalled the women were compelled "to bear heavy burdens and plod our weary way with our feet entirely naked, through snow to the depth of 2, 3 and 4 feet." They dressed like American Indian women, did menial tasks around the camp such as carrying water, and were fed little food. They were under constant threat of an Indian ambush; however, after the brutal murder of her family and her own suffering as a captive, Abbie Gardner did not care if she lived or died.[53]

Gardner survived but Elizabeth Thatcher did not. Still recovering from her pregnancy and mourning the murder of her baby, Thatcher grew increasingly ill. Her breasts were swollen, and one leg swelled and turned black. Thatcher was young, only nineteen years old, but the journey had left her sick, exhausted, and unable to travel quickly. Conditions worsened for the entire band when the supply of food stolen in the raids ran low and the village was forced to start eating the horses. By the time the band reached the Big Sioux River in South Dakota, members were frustrated with Thatcher's slow progress. As she struggled to cross the river on a fallen log, she fell into the water. Somehow Thatcher made it to shore, only to be clubbed to death by the Dakotas, who then pushed her body back into the river.[54]

By May Inkpaduta had reached the James River. While good weather and better food sources, including buffalo, helped, the band had only one horse remaining. Inkpaduta set up his village on Skunk Lake, near present-day Madison, South Dakota. Inkpaduta was still with the band ten days later, when two Christian Dakotas came to his lodge wanting to trade for the women prisoners.[55]

The territorial legislature of Minnesota had authorized ten thousand dollars to obtain the release of the captured women. There was still hope they could be rescued. On May 6 the *St. Peter Courier* reported that a friendly Dakota man, who encountered Inkpaduta at the Rock River, had learned the women were fatigued but alive. Encouraged, Flandrau recruited two Christian Wahpetons, Sounding Heavens and Gray Foot, to attempt to win the release of the women. Arriving at Skunk Lake, Sounding Heavens and Gray Foot met with Inkpaduta. At first Inkpaduta suspected the two Christians were actually scouts for an army expedition preparing to attack him. Sounding Heavens criticized Inkpaduta for killing the settlers, insisting Inkpaduta would pay for the massacre. He added it would not be fair for other innocent Dakotas to suffer along with him. If Inkpaduta released the women to them, Sounding Heavens argued, perhaps the whites would take this as an act of good faith and not punish the Dakotas. Inkpaduta proudly replied that his actions were so daring and outrageous, he would not be harmed by the ineffectual whites. Nevertheless, after a long night of discussions, Inkpaduta agreed to release one woman to protect other Dakotas from reprisals.[56]

The two men chose Margaret Marble. Marble was older than the other two captives and appeared to be more worn-out by the ordeal. In return, Inkpaduta received several horses plus powder and lead. On May 21 the two liberators presented a free Margaret Marble to Flandrau. For their services, Sounding Heavens and Gray Foot received five hundred dollars in gold and a promise of another five hundred dollars from Flandrau.[57]

Following Marble's release, Inkpaduta moved his band back to the James River. Near the confluence of the James and Snake Rivers, he joined a large Yankton encampment of two hundred lodges. In late May Inkpaduta sold Lydia Nobles and Abbie Gardner to End of the Snake, a one-legged Yankton man with a crutch. Soon after, in June, Roaring Cloud came to End of the Snake's village wanting sex with Lydia Nobles. Nobles, age twenty, was a strong woman who had refused to give in to her captors; she had fought back on a number of occasions. When Roaring Cloud entered the lodge in which Nobles and Gardner were housed, he ordered Nobles to come outside with him. She refused to leave the lodge. Enraged, Roaring Cloud pulled her from the lodge and beat her to death with a piece of firewood; it took her more than half an hour to die. The next day, Gardner saw Lydia's body being used for target practice.[58]

Having successfully arranged the release of Margaret Marble, Flandrau asked three more Dakota men — Paul Mazakutamane, John Other Day, and Iron Hawk — to undertake the rescue of Gardner. Who Shoots Metal as He Walks (also known as Little Paul or Paul Mazakutamane) was a Christian convert and president of the Hazelwood Republic. He had cut his hair short, wore white men's clothing, and claimed, "I was born an Indian, but now I considered myself a white man." John Other Day also converted to Christianity after he killed three or four band members in a violent, drunken brawl.[59] The three men agreed to find Gardner.

Setting out on May 23, they journeyed to present-day South Dakota and discovered Nobles's body six days later. After burying Lydia Nobles, they met with Inkpaduta while he was still living with the Yanktons. Inkpaduta's camp had diminished, consisting of only three lodges. Inkpaduta and his sons may have had a disagreement over future plans. His sons and their followers had left the village. They favored more raids and staying closer to the traditional Dakota lands; Inkpaduta wanted to live farther west among the Yanktons, away from the vengeful whites. Negotiations for Gardner's release lasted three days before a bargain was reached: End of the Snake sold Gardner for two horses, seven blankets, two kegs of gunpowder, one box of to-bacco, and a few sundry items.[60]

The three men put Gardner in a wagon. Escorted by the two sons of End of the Snake, they reached the Upper Sioux Agency on June 10. The *Fairbault Herald* described the freed Gardner as "very sun burnt and resembles in complexion, very strikingly, her late tawny associates." On June 23 the three rescuers re-ceived twelve hundred dollars for their mission of mercy.[61]

The release of Gardner ended the events of the Spirit Lake massacre. But the effects of the attacks would be felt for many years to come. Inkpaduta remained unpunished and, following Gardner's rescue, was seen again by few white men. He slipped away into the vast regions of the West. To whites, he was a savage, ready to strike or reappear anywhere and at any time. The real-life Inkpaduta was now replaced by a frontier bogeyman who could be blamed for any wrong deed, crime, or violent act per-petrated against settlers in Iowa or Minnesota even though it is likely he never returned to Iowa and rarely ventured into Minnesota.

Inkpaduta left behind him a frontier tense with suspicion. Relations between the settlers and the Dakotas worsened after the massacre and remained troubled through the Dakota War of 1862. Some settlers advocated removing the Dakotas from Min-nesota, while a few whites wanted to wipe out the tribe altogether. Christian Dakotas, attempting to assimilate into white civiliza-tion, condemned Inkpaduta as an outlaw who was hated by his people. But secretly many Dakotas were sympathetic to Ink-paduta, including those who approved of his raids. Because of kinship ties, many were willing to protect him. Joseph Brown, an

Indian agent following Flandrau, summed up the situation in a report to the Commissioner of Indian Affairs: "The failure to pursue and punish Inkpaduta and his band for the wholesale murder of our citizens at Spirit Lake has confirmed them [Dakotas] in the belief that the government is weak and can not punish Indian aggressions."[62] The failure to apprehend Inkpaduta would come back to haunt the U.S. military.

CHAPTER 6

# *"If They Resist"*

## RETRIBUTION AND NEW CONFLICTS

Inkpaduta had faded into the West, disappearing from the view of whites. His vanishing, however, did not end the desire of the military and others to punish him for the massacre. Because Inkpaduta eluded capture, retribution came instead to members of his family. Mainly, these reprisals were caused by other Dakotas, thus once again convincing American Indians of the weakness of the whites who constantly failed to apprehend Inkpaduta. Many people of the time, as well as historians, believe the failure to capture Inkpaduta was an important factor in the instigation of the Dakota War of 1862.

On the northwestern frontier, any crime or act of violence caused by an unknown American Indian was blamed on Inkpaduta. He was said to be raiding from the Canadian border down to Kansas, as well as throughout northern Iowa and southern Minnesota. "Wherever an outrage was committed the tracks of the bloody-handed chief might have been found nearby," wrote Robinson.[1] If a horse was stolen or an isolated settler was murdered, the culprit was assumed to be Inkpaduta, even without the word of eyewitnesses. Christian Indians damned him out of hand, while other Sioux found him a convenient scapegoat for any misdeeds they felt could cause them trouble with the whites, especially after the failed Dakota War of 1862.

The Dakota War brought new accusations against Inkpaduta. He was said to be one of the key instigators behind the uprising. Robinson claimed, "His hands were among the bloodiest," and Clodfelter believed that "from Spirit Lake to the last battles of the badlands, Inkpaduta was present, in spirit if not always in body instigating, inflaming."[2] Inkpaduta was said to have participated in another massacre at Lake Shetek along with Joshpaduta. He was also believed to have fought in other engagements of the conflict.

After the defeat of the Dakotas, the army pursued the surviving resisters onto the plains of the Dakota Territory. Here they encountered not only the Dakotas but also the Yanktons and Lakotas. Some writers have made Inkpaduta into a commander in chief of the Sioux in the battles that followed,. No longer was he merely an outlaw leader of a small band of malcontents; Inkpaduta would be viewed as a champion of Sioux independence. Van Nuys argued that Inkpaduta organized the resistance to the army and led the allied Sioux forces in the 1863 and 1864 battles and campaigns. Herriot referred to Inkpaduta as the "evil genius of the Sioux." Lee credited Inkpaduta's new high standing with the Sioux to "his hatred for the whites, his revengeful disposition, and his nearly matchless success in war."[3]

Yet, following the massacre, Inkpaduta stayed well away from white settlements, living with the Yanktons along the James River in present-day South Dakota. Robinson maintained that "when an Indian had rendered himself obnoxious to the whites or to his tribe so that life was unsafe on the frontier, he knew that a welcome ever awaited him in the lodges of the desperado." However, it was during this time that Inkpaduta's band divided. His two sons, Roaring Cloud and Fire Cloud, moved back to Min-

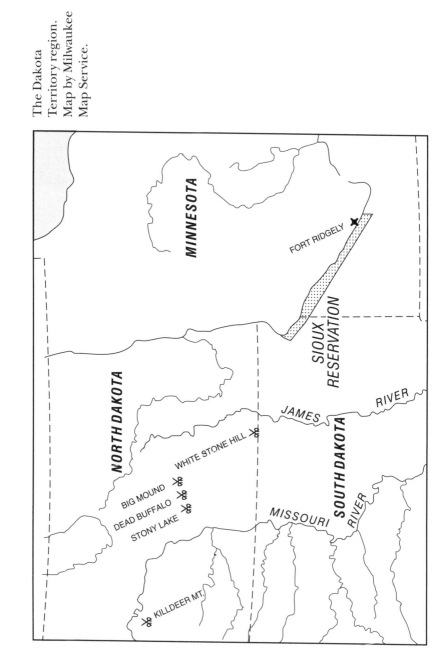

The Dakota Territory region. Map by Milwaukee Map Service.

MINNESOTA

FORT RIDGELY

SIOUX RESERVATION

NORTH DAKOTA

JAMES RIVER

WHITE STONE HILL

BIG MOUND
DEAD BUFFALO
STONY LAKE

SOUTH DAKOTA

MISSOURI RIVER

KILLDEER MT.

nesota either to continue raiding the settlers or to be near other Dakotas on the reservation — or perhaps both. In June 1857 local trader Joseph Brown wrote to the *Henderson Democrat* that the two sons were within two miles of Fort Ridgely inciting the Dakotas to "acts of hostility." He complained that while this was happening, the soldiers at the post were "very quietly and efficiently eating their bread and pork within the walls."[4]

On July 2 Flandrau received reliable information from Sam Brown, another reservation trader, that part of Inkpaduta's band was on the reservation. Unknown to him at the time, it was Roaring Cloud and his new wife who had come to visit her family. Roaring Cloud and three to six lodges were encamped five miles above the Upper Sioux Agency near Sleepy Eye's village. Flandrau immediately requested military support from Fort Ridgely. Lieutenant Murray and fifteen soldiers traveled the thirteen miles to the Lower Sioux Agency in wagons, arriving around 5:00 P.M. Flandrau met the detachment with twelve mounted white volunteers armed with shotguns and pistols from the reservation and John Other Day as a guide.[5]

Led by John Other Day, Murray and Flandrau marched thirty miles; they crossed the Yellow Medicine River, arriving near Roaring Cloud's camp at daylight. The village was located on the prairie near the bluffs of the river. Realizing the bluffs were a possible escape route, Murray split his command into two squads and moved them into a blocking position along the stream. Meanwhile, Flandrau and his mounted volunteers advanced directly on the sleeping camp. Since the weather was warm, the Dakotas had rolled up the hides on their lodges to allow the air to flow through. This allowed someone to notice and give warning of Flandrau's impending advance two hundred yards away from the village. Villagers began to run, including Roaring Cloud and his wife. The volunteers opened fire with their shotguns, but the distance was too great for much accuracy. Roaring Cloud rushed into a ravine — as Murray expected — and encountered the waiting soldiers. Firing a shotgun at the waiting soldiers four times, Roaring Cloud fought for his life. Returning fire, the soldiers wounded him multiple times. A soldier finally crept into the ravine and killed Roaring Cloud with a bayonet.[6]

Hoping to obtain information, Flandrau had Roaring Cloud's widow and child taken prisoner. This was done despite the objections of Murray, who believed their abduction would lead to trouble. The detachment then headed back to the Upper Sioux Agency. Tensions were high at the agency, with a pending annuity payment and large numbers of Yanktons and Yanktonais demanding to share in the distribution of money and supplies. As Murray and Flandrau rode toward the agency, they passed through the villages. Roaring Cloud's widow began to yell to the Nakotas for help. When Murray, Flandrau, and their men stopped at the Daniels's boardinghouse for breakfast, the house was soon surrounded by an angry mob demanding the release of the woman. Murray was forced to release the prisoners and provide two cows to the besiegers.[7]

Murray sent a messenger to Fort Ridgely to request relief. On July 6 Maj. Thomas Sherman and twenty-five soldiers arrived at the agency after marching forty-five miles in twenty-four hours. The situation remained serious, with a soldier stabbed and Sherman threatening to burn down a village, before more troops arrived on July 15 and 16. Encouraged by the killing of Roaring Cloud, Stephen Riggs, a missionary to the Dakotas, urged Flandrau to quickly mount a further expedition to obtain the rest of Inkpaduta's band "before they have killed more whites." Riggs offered to raise a company of men for Flandrau's use.[8]

Tensions were not eased by the arrival of Superintendent William Cullen, who was in charge of distributing the annuity. On July 19 Cullen, under orders from Washington, informed the Dakotas that there would be no payment until Inkpaduta was arrested or killed by the Dakotas themselves. Angry at this unjust demand, the chiefs argued against the denial of the annuity.

Standing Buffalo complained to Cullen, "Our Great Father has asked us to do a very hard thing . . . to go and kill men and women that do not belong to our bands." A nervous and inexperienced Cullen, who Joseph Brown said could not tell the difference between "a Sioux Indian and a snapping turtle," telegraphed Commissioner of Indian Affairs James Denver a weak message: "What should I do?" Denver firmly responded, "Adhere to your instructions; there will be no yielding." Encouraged, Cullen told the Dakota leaders they had two choices: mount an expedition against Inkpaduta or face war with the United States.[9]

With few options, Little Crow, a Mdewakanton chieftain, agreed to lead an expedition against Inkpaduta. He requested support from the army; however, Major Sherman declined to send any men, fearing treachery from the Dakotas. The military did agree to provide a wagon to carry supplies. On July 22 Little Crow and one hundred men (mainly Sissetons and Wahpetons from the pro-assimilation group), plus six mixed-bloods, and white interpreter Antoine Campbell, left the Upper Sioux Agency.[10]

The expedition reached Skunk Lake on July 28. They discovered two small abandoned camps totaling six lodges and a trail leading to Lake Herman, which was ten to twelve miles away. Approaching Lake Herman, Little Crow encountered eight men, nine women, and a dozen children standing in the reeds of the lake. After Little Crow's group called to them to come out and greet their party as friends, two women and a child went out to Little Crow. After shaking hands and talking briefly, the women returned to their band members and informed them the Dakotas were not friendly. A skirmish followed as both sides opened fire. In a running battle that lasted more than half an hour, until nightfall and a rainstorm broke off the pursuit, Little Crow's men killed three men, wounded another, and captured two women and one child. Little Crow learned from the captured women that one of the dead men was Fire Cloud, Inkpaduta's son. He had been killed by John Other Day. The other two dead men were Shifting Wind and His Mysterious Feather, who were both members of Inkpaduta's band and participants in the Spirit Lake massacre.[11]

On August 5 Little Crow returned to the Upper Sioux Agency with his prisoners. Pleased with the results, Bureau of Indian Affairs officials tried to get another expedition to take the field, but they ran into solid resistance from the Sioux. The Dakotas felt they had done what was expected of them. Acting Commissioner of Indian Affairs Charles Mix agreed and ordered the previously withheld annuity to be distributed.[12]

The military had also been planning a campaign against Inkpaduta. Upon the news of Abbie Gardner's release, Flandrau and Colonel Alexander started preparations for a major offensive. It was intended to be a multiple-pronged attack involving five companies of regulars. In July the *St. Paul Pioneer and Democrat* announced the arrival of four companies of the Second Infantry at Fort Ridgely. Coming from Fort Randall on the Missouri River, they were to spearhead the campaign against Inkpaduta. The expedition never happened, however, as most of the Fort Ridgely garrison was soon ordered to the west to participate in the so-called Mormon War in Utah.[13]

Territorial governor Samuel Medary, disappointed with the lackluster performance of the army, proposed to raise a volunteer cavalry force in Minnesota to hunt for Inkpaduta. He requested permission and support from Secretary of War John Floyd but was denied.[14]

Limited military patrols continued the search for Inkpaduta. In September 1857 Little Crow served as scout for Companies G and L of the Second Artillery as they conducted a search of the Coteau des Prairies area west of Fort Ridgely. The patrol passed through the Pipestone quarries and then overland to Lake Benton before returning to the post empty-handed. A smaller detachment commanded by a Lieutenant Smalley checked out a rumor that Inkpaduta's band was encamped on either Timber or Skunk Lake. At Timber Lake, a friendly Dakota told Smalley Inkpaduta was not there but could be found at Lake Shetek or along the Big Cottonwood River. A Lieutenant Outler scouted both areas, advancing fifteen miles up the Big Cottonwood River but discovering no sign of Inkpaduta.[15]

In October a Lieutenant Ruggles received the following orders from his captain, Alfred Sully: "You will proceed with your command to the camp of Sleepy Eye. . . . You will arrive at the camp as early as you can in the morning. . . . On arriving at the camp you will so place your men that you may be able to cut off any retreat, while a demand is made of Sleepy Eye for two of Inkpaduta's band said to be there." No evidence of Inkpaduta was discovered, but Sleepy Eye was beaten and brought back to the fort under arrest.[16]

As with so much of Inkpaduta's life, it is not known what he was doing during late 1857. It can be assumed he was mourning the death of his older sons, and there were reports that he came into Minnesota to bury Roaring Cloud in the traditional Dakota fashion. Another rumor contended he was heading west to join the Cheyennes in their opposition to a punitive military expedition. In August a panic occurred among settlers and Upper Sioux reservation employees when they believed Inkpaduta was at nearby Wood Lake with the Yanktons. Whites remained on the alert all through the night, fearing an attack. In the fall, there were several Indian raids against the town of Sioux Falls; Inkpaduta was blamed for the loss of a yoke of oxen taken during one raid.[17]

In the summer of 1858 whites' hopes were raised when several newspapers reported Inkpaduta's capture. In June the *Sioux City Eagle* declared that "the celebrated Indian Inkpaduta has been captured" on the prairie close to the city. Other accounts stated Inkpaduta was taken at St. Peter and on the Yellow Medicine

River above Fort Ridgely; all these stories were false.[18] Soon new allegations of raids by Inkpaduta emerged.

In what would soon be the Dakota Territory, Inkpaduta was said to have raided the town of Medary and stolen three horses at Sioux Falls.[19] As with many such claims of attacks on whites, there is a lack of hard evidence or eyewitness accounts of Inkpaduta committing the acts attributed to him, and most—perhaps all—of these claims were likely false. If unknown American Indians stole horses or livestock, or killed a white man, people believed the culprit was Inkpaduta. Any suspicious American Indian found lurking nearby was anointed "Inkpaduta" by fearful settlers.

In Iowa there were claims of Inkpaduta's return to Spirit Lake, the scene of his actual crime. In February 1858 a frontier guard confirmed seeing him around the lake. On March 4 the *Hamilton Freeman* announced to its readers that Inkpaduta was prowling around Spirit Lake. The paper followed this report three weeks later with a new story of men finding evidence that Inkpaduta's band were in the vicinity. A rumor surfaced in November that insisted Abbie Gardner had recognized members of Inkpaduta's band in the area.[20]

In reality, Inkpaduta was probably still encamped with the Yanktons along the James River. This became a favorite area of his during the years prior to the Dakota War of 1862. Yet, even along the James, Inkpaduta was affected by the encroachment of white settlement. In 1851 the Dakotas had sold their lands to the federal government, and by 1858 the government wanted to purchase land from the Yanktons. Once more, the frontier was moving westward, and settlers were interested in the territory between the Big Sioux River and the Missouri River. On April 19 the nonresistant Yanktons signed the Treaty of Washington. Under this treaty the Yanktons sold 11,155,890 acres of their lands for $1.6 million in annuity payments to be spread out over fifty years, retaining only 400,000 acres for a reservation. Both the

Lakotas and Yanktonais had claims to the relinquished lands, which had been sold without their approval. This caused great anger toward the Yanktons. The Dakota Territory was organized soon after, and on July 10, 1859, it was officially thrown open for settlement.[21] Inkpaduta was forced to move away from the Yanktons, thus to live more often with the Yanktonais.

In 1859 a new report of a capture emerged; however, this story concerned members of Inkpaduta's band rather than Inkpaduta himself. In August a story in the *St. Peter Free Press* stated that Major Sherman had captured two men belonging to Inkpaduta's village. Caught near New Ulm, Minnesota, one was being held in that town, while the other was taken to Fort Ridgely. The prisoners were to be tried by civil authorities. The editor questioned this plan, adding, "We must say that we don't understand the necessity for any such formal and expensive proceedings. They are a set of as villainous outlaws as ever cursed the earth; and they ought to be shot down at once, wherever and whenever found."[22]

Fear of new Inkpaduta attacks surfaced when Joseph Brown, the new Indian agent, related a rumor that the renegade chieftain was set to invade the state. That fall, Governor Henry H. Sibley wrote excitedly to Maj. W.W. Morris, commander at Fort Ridgely. Sibley pleaded for military aid for settlers at Belmont, Minnesota, who allegedly were being slaughtered by hordes of murdering Indians. Morris sent Capt. John Pemberton and Company F, Fourth Artillery, to the area. Upon their arrival, they found frightened but quite safe settlers — and no Dakotas. Sibley later wrote Morris apologizing for the false alarm and thanking him for his assistance.[23]

Not all whites were terrified of the reputedly omnipresent Inkpaduta. One man from Georgetown, Dakota Territory, who knew that fear of Inkpaduta was making settlers abandon the new territory, wrote a letter to the *St. Cloud Democrat*. He called Inkpaduta "a great bugbear" and a "blind old man" who only wanted "to remain squatted in his lodge and getting his dried buffalo meat regularly, than making warlike speeches in council, or preparing to follow the warpath."[24] But most believed that Inkpaduta was a real threat and that he was prepared to make constant war along the frontier.

In 1861 Inkpaduta was blamed for a double murder. That April, William Tubbs of New Ulm went missing and was believed dead; and John Reinackes was killed on the Cottonwood River. The *Scott County Record* noted, "Inkpaduta's band is said to be on the outskirts of the settlement." Again, there were no eyewitnesses.[25]

Regardless of whether or not Inkpaduta was involved in raiding, 1861 would be an important year for the frontier. With the commencement of the Civil War, regular soldiers were removed from their posts in the West and sent east to defeat the Southern rebellion. Volunteer state regiments replaced these soldiers, taking up their duties of protecting incoming settlers, keeping the peace, and in Minnesota, overseeing the reservation. Companies from several Minnesota regiments served at Fort Ridgely over the next few years.

While the regulars departed, rumors of Inkpaduta's raiding continued to persist. These included claims from the new Indian agent for the reservation, Thomas Galbraith. Galbraith was an ineffectual bigot who received the position as a reward for supporting the Republicans in the 1860 elections. Galbraith reported to Superintendent Clark Thompson that twenty to thirty horses were stolen off the reservation. He fixed responsibility for the thefts on "the more daring outlaws of different bands, pupils . . . of Inkpaduta and White Lodge."[26] White Lodge was another Dakota renegade who was often linked with Inkpaduta. Meanwhile, settlers at Spirit Lake again claimed Inkpaduta was in the area. A company of fifty soldiers under a Captain Western proceeded to the lake country but found no sign of Indians.[27]

After many false stories concerning his whereabouts in Iowa or

Minnesota, Inkpaduta did venture back toward Minnesota in mid-1862. In early summer Inkpaduta led his band away from the Yanktonais and journeyed to Lake Benton near the Minnesota border. It has been postulated that Inkpaduta was attempting to obtain part of the upcoming annuity payment, perhaps through kinship ties with the Wahpekutes or Sissetons. Along the way one of his sons (likely Big Face) led a raiding party that encountered three white men, named Greenway, Lamb, and Brown; the men were riding in two wagons. The war party stole one of the wagons and its team before leaving. Soon after, Brown happened to spend the night in Inkpaduta's village and noticed the wagon and team. If this account is true, the supposedly bloodthirsty Inkpaduta was not killing every white man he found.[28]

Brown, upset with the theft, made his way to the Upper Sioux Agency and informed Galbraith of Inkpaduta's presence. This was the second warning the Indian agent had received; previously, on June 2, missionary Thomas S. Williamson had written Galbraith that he had learned one of Inkpaduta's sons was close to the reservation, stealing horses and planning to demand part of the annuity payment.[29]

Galbraith already had a serious problem on his hands. More than four thousand Sissetons and Wahpetons were waiting for their provisions as part of the annuity; however, the annuity was late, and the Indian agent would not release any supplies to the near-starving people until the payment arrived. As tensions increased, Galbraith requested troops from Fort Ridgely. Lt. Timothy Sheehan and two companies of the Fifth Minnesota Infantry regiment, (approximately one hundred men) were dispatched to the Upper Sioux Agency to keep the peace. Galbraith instructed Sheehan to organize an expedition to capture Inkpaduta, ordering him to "take said Inkpaduta and all of the Indian soldiers with him, prisoners, alive if possible and deliver them at the agency." Galbraith added: "If they resist I advise that they be shot."[30]

On July 28 Sheehan left the agency with fourteen soldiers, four civilian volunteers, and a scout named Good Voiced Hail mounted on mules. Good Voiced Hail guided them to a small lake close to Lake Benton, where Sheehan found an old camp-site with wagon tracks leading away onto the prairie. The soldiers followed the tracks, which eventually disappeared near a grove. Believing Inkpaduta was in the grove, Sheehan ordered a charge into the woods but encountered no one. Warned of Sheehan's mission by kinsmen and friends, Inkpaduta fled back to the Dakota Territory. Disappointed, the lieutenant returned to the agency on August 3. Inkpaduta's status with his people rose once again. Sheehan's inability to capture Inkpaduta—yet another failure by the military—only aggravated the problem at the agency. The Dakotas, convinced of the soldiers' weakness to op-pose them, decided to take the supplies due them from the agency warehouses.[31]

Sheehan performed more ably in defusing the crisis at the agency. When he first arrived at the agency, Sheehan had con-vinced Galbraith to release some of the food he was holding in the warehouses. On August 4, sure that the army could not stop them, four hundred to eight hundred warriors rushed the ware-houses, breaking in and distributing the food to their hungry families. Sheehan reacted quickly. He forced the men from the buildings with threats and armed soldiers. Capt. John Marsh, commander at Fort Ridgely, arrived soon after; he supported Sheehan's action and ordered Galbraith to turn the food in the warehouses over to the Dakotas. Having received their food, the Sissetons and Wahpetons were willing to disperse back to their villages to await the tardy annuity money.[32] Though successful in averting a war at the Upper Sioux Agency, Marsh failed to stop an uprising at the Lower Sioux Agency, the event that led to the Dakota War of 1862.

There are several reasons why a majority of the Dakotas went to war in 1862. Bitterness over the treaties of 1851 and the Treaty of 1858 was a major cause of the conflict, along with the failure of the U.S. government to live up to its obligations under the treaties. Other contributing factors, which arose once the Dakotas were living on the reservations, included outrageous prices charged by traders at their stores that resulted in increasing debt and assimilation efforts by the Indian agents and missionaries that disrupted their traditional communal bonds — not to mention the continual encroachments of white settlers who surrounded the reservations and openly showed their prejudice toward American Indians. The loss of hunting and trapping left the Dakotas hungry and directly threatened their traditional culture.[33]

More immediate reasons for the war included the destruction of the 1861 corn crop by cutworms, which brought the Dakotas to the verge of starvation, and the tardiness of the annuity, the result of a lack of gold coins needed to make the payment because of the Southern rebellion. The outbreak of the Civil War convinced the Dakotas that with so many young white men away fighting the Confederacy, few remained to oppose the Sioux. This heightened the desire of young warriors to make war for glory and to achieve a return to the traditional life of the Dakotas.[34]

Inkpaduta influenced both long- and short-term causes for the war. Numerous eyewitnesses to the conflict, as well as later writers and historians, considered him an important motivator of the Dakotas. For five years, prior to the Dakota War, the army and white government officials had repeatedly tried to capture or kill Inkpaduta but failed miserably. Their failure, coupled with the fact many Dakotas approved of his attacks on Spirit Lake and Springfield, made him a hero. Inkpaduta had successfully led a revenge raid in the best warmaking tradition of his people. He also had opposed the selling of the Dakotas' land and remained firmly wedded to the traditional culture of the Sioux. The rest of the Santees had submitted to existence on a reservation they hated, but not Inkpaduta; he was still living free. Further, it seemed he had exposed the weakness of the whites and proved that a war of revenge and liberation against them could be victorious.[35]

The Dakota War of 1862 started with a murder. On August 17, 1861, four young Dakota men murdered five settlers near Acton, Minnesota. Fleeing back to the Lower Sioux Agency, they told others about their crime. After lengthy discussions that lasted into the early morning hours of the eighteenth, many Wahpe-kute and Mdewakanton leaders, including a reluctant Little Crow, decided on war. Later that morning, warriors attacked the Lower Sioux Agency and killed all the whites they encountered. After hearing of the assault from terrified civilians escaping to Fort Ridgely, Captain Marsh led most of the seventy-eight-man garrison out of the post intending to quell the rebellion. Instead, the Dakotas ambushed him at Redwood Ferry as he tried to cross the river. They killed Marsh, along with twenty-three men under his command. The survivors made their way back to the fort as Dakota war parties spread out to raid the unsuspecting settlers.[36]

Several stories describe how Little Crow plotted the war well in advance with the help of Inkpaduta. Little Crow, some writers have said, was inspired to revolt by Inkpaduta's attacks on the whites and summoned him for advice and counsel. This was reportedly why Inkpaduta returned to Minnesota prior to Shee-han's attempt to capture him. On Sunday, August 17, Inkpaduta, Little Crow, and Little Priest, who was a warlike Ho-Chunk, sup-posedly went to church together — an ominous sign of the con-spiracy.[37]

Clearly these accounts are fiction. When he was first told of the Acton murders, Little Crow did not want to go to war and argued against it. Little Crow had no long-term plot to attack the whites. Once the war began, as they did with Inkpaduta, whites would brand Little Crow the leader of the uprising and a savage warmonger.

Dakota warriors struck against the unassuming and defenseless settlers, killing approximately five hundred people. They committed atrocities including murder, rape, and looting. These actions were no different than those perpetrated by Inkpaduta five years earlier. These raids also targeted men, women, and children. The causes for the war were similar to those that motivated Inkpaduta to act: hunger, white bigotry, and serious personal and cultural loss.

Expansion of the war was effectively blocked by two events: the failure of the Dakotas to capture Fort Ridgely in two assaults on August 20 and 22, and their inability to take the city of New Ulm (although by the end of the fighting, the town was almost totally destroyed). Fort Ridgely appeared vulnerable after the demise of Marsh and his command; but timely reinforcements and veteran artillerymen manning the cannons defeated Little Crow's attempts to overwhelm the garrison. On August 23, at New Ulm, civilians from the town and militiamen from St. Peter fought off the Dakotas in a fierce contest for control of the town. The two Dakota losses ended the first stage of the war.

While Waggoner and Eastman, both Dakotas, stated that Inkpaduta participated in the war, it is likely that he was not present at the opening events of the conflict. Inkpaduta was still living along the James River when war broke out. He moved to the Yellow Medicine River after he received word of the fighting. Waggoner believed it was Little Crow himself who informed Inkpaduta hoping he would join the conflict.[38]

Having committed one massacre, Inkpaduta was readily accused by Robinson and other writers of taking part in another, the well-known Lake Shetek massacre. On August 20 a war party attacked Lake Shetek, a community of forty to fifty people located seventy miles west of Mankato. They killed fifteen people, wounded many, and took several prisoners. Robinson asserted that Inkpaduta had carried out the raid. However, both survivors and participants in the massacre clearly indicated the leader was

Lean Bear, a member of White Lodge's village. No primary evidence ties Inkpaduta to the massacre or even claims he was there.[39]

One of the prisoners taken at Lake Shetek was a Mrs. Dudley, who was released at the end of the war. She remembered meeting in the Dakota Territory one of Inkpaduta's sons, perhaps Big Face. Big Face told her that his band had had little to do with the fighting up to that point but would be more involved in the spring.[40] Based on this account, Inkpaduta even then was not a main leader of the Dakotas as postulated by Robinson, Clodfelter and others. The leaders of the uprising were well-known band chieftains such as Little Crow; their roles in the war have been well documented.[41] If Inkpaduta did indeed fight in this war, he did so only in the final battles of the conflict.

The Americans seized the offensive when Col. Henry H. Sibley, an ex-trader and former governor of Minnesota, led fifteen hundred soldiers, mainly militia but backed by the Sixth Minnesota Infantry, into the valley. His force relieved Fort Ridgely on August 28. Several battles and skirmishes followed that quickly left the Dakotas overwhelmed. Some started to surrender and gathered at Camp Release along with the many Dakotas who had never favored war and took no part in the fighting.[42]

By this point Inkpaduta was involved in the war. During September 3–6, he took part in the short siege of Fort Abercrombie in present-day North Dakota before joining the main force of resisters under Little Crow. The decisive battle of the war came at Wood Lake. On September 23, seven hundred warriors—including Inkpaduta—attempted to ambush Sibley's army. They were discovered by a party of the Third Minnesota Infantry, which consisted of veteran fighters recently paroled by their Confederate captors. A fierce engagement occurred, with both sides mounting charges before the Dakotas were forced to give up the field. This loss demoralized the resisters, and large numbers surrendered to the army.[43]

   Little Crow and five hundred to eight hundred Mdewakantons and Wahpekutes fled the area. They headed onto the plains
of the Dakota Territory where twenty-eight hundred Sissetons
and Wahpetons — not necessarily participants in the war — were
dwelling. The majority of the Dakotas were banished from Minnesota. They lost their reservation and were sent farther west to a
new reservation on the Missouri River one hundred miles from
Fort Randall. Other Dakotas were arrested for war crimes; a
vengeful military court sentenced 303 to death. President Lincoln reduced this number to 38, but those sentenced still included several innocent men. They were hanged on December 26 in Mankato. Because of Inkpaduta's notoriety as a source
of true evil, some writers asserted that all 38, or at least some of
the men, were members of Inkpaduta's band. Linking atrocities
committed by the Dakotas to Inkpaduta was becoming common-
place. Robinson claimed that Inkpaduta was constantly raiding
throughout the area and implicated him in the killings of Amos
Huggins at Lac Qui Parle, some haymakers at Big Stone, and
Judge Amidon and his son at Sioux Falls. "Wherever he appeared," wrote Robinson, "murder and theft marked his trail."[44]
In the fall of 1862 Inkpaduta was said to also have been involved
in a skirmish at Sioux Falls.
   At the start of the Dakota War, the citizens of Sioux Falls left
their vulnerable community for the safety of more settled areas.
On November 1 Capt. Nelson Miner and eleven soldiers of Company A, First Dakota Cavalry, escorted a party of six civilians back
to Sioux Falls. The civilians hoped to retrieve household goods
and other property they had buried when they evacuated the
town. They reached Sioux Falls on the evening of November 2.
The next morning Miner was making breakfast when he noticed
riders in the distance. Realizing the riders were Sioux, Miner and
Corp. Joe Ellis, who served as an interpreter, rode out to the
Indians, who had retreated into a nearby ravine. Four men
emerged from the ravine when Miner called to them to come

out and talk. Miner tried to find out their purpose for being in
the area and where they were from. The warriors responded with
gestures of defiance and threats. Growing impatient, Miner
pulled his pistol and began to fire. The warriors returned to the
ravine.

As Miner's men raced to his assistance, a dozen Dakotas
opened fire from cover. Miner ordered a charge into the ravine
that scattered the warriors onto the prairie. The soldiers pursued the Indians in a running battle for two miles. Inkpaduta's
nephew Wakeyandota (Red Lightning), who was described as "a
giant of an Indian," leaped from his horse; he beckoned his men
to stand and fight. Unfortunately for Red Lightning, no one saw
him dismount so the Dakotas continued to retreat, leaving him
isolated. With Red Lightning soon engulfed by the charging
soldiers, a wild melee ensued. Red Lightning fired a double-
barreled shotgun at Corp. Ellis but missed his target. Swinging
his empty weapon as a club, Red Lightning swung at Ellis, who
parried the blow with a saber, breaking the gun stock. A private, named Gray, fired at Red Lightning. Falling to his knees
wounded, Red Lightning pulled a knife and stabbed at Ellis,
injuring the soldier's horse in the neck. Ellis finally killed the
Dakota with his saber. Meanwhile, realizing what had happened,
other warriors were firing on the soldiers from nearby woods.
Miner ordered a withdrawal after allowing his men to scalp
Red Lightning and set fire to the prairie grass to cover their
retreat.[45]

Men involved in the skirmish and the first newspaper story
that was based on eyewitness accounts never mentioned Inkpaduta as being present—only his nephew, Red Lightning. It was
only later that Robinson and other writers stated Inkpaduta and
forty of his men were present in Sioux Falls for the skirmish. In
fact, by December Inkpaduta was encamped one hundred miles
north of Fort Pierre, living with the exiled Dakotas.[46]

These exiled Dakotas remained a threat to the settlers living on the frontier. War parties raided Minnesota and limited white expansion into the Dakota Territory. The Dakotas further harassed gold miners traveling up the Missouri River to the mines in Montana. In 1863 and 1864 the military mounted expeditions against the Dakotas, enlarging the war to include the Yanktonais and the Lakotas. The Yanktons took no part in the fighting. With these campaigns, Inkpaduta's status was raised to new heights as the Lakotas and Yanktonais viewed him as a leader of the resisters and a Sioux hero at large for fighting the encroaching whites. Inkpaduta was becoming something of a national patriot defending his people from their enemies. Based on this respect for Inkpaduta, many whites have exaggerated his role in later battles.

In the summer of 1863 two military columns—one commanded by Gen. Alfred Sully, a forty-three-year-old career officer sympathetic to American Indians and their poor treatment on the reservations; and the second led by the newly promoted General Sibley—moved against the Sioux. The two columns were to act as a pincer, to trap the hostile Sioux between them. By this time, Little Crow was dead, having been killed by a farmer while picking berries with his son in Minnesota.[47] This incident again made Inkpaduta the leading opponent in the minds of settlers and the army.

Sibley with 2,200 infantry and 800 cavalry, plus artillery, pioneers, and scouts, left Fort Ridgely and headed west into the Dakota Territory. Sibley engaged the Sioux in three battles—at Big Mound, Dead Buffalo Lake, and Stoney Lake. Coming up from the south, Sully's column, consisting of 1,200 cavalry and 325 infantry troops, battled the Sioux at Whitestone Hill. Several Internet sites, including the site for the American Battlefield Protection Program, list Inkpaduta as the overall commander of the Sioux forces at all four battles. Clodfelter and Van Nuys presented Inkpaduta in this role as well.[48] To them, Inkpaduta had become a leader who transcended village, tribe, band, and divisional leadership. They claimed that the Lakotas, Yanktonais, and Dakotas all viewed him with great respect as a military commander and turned overall military leadership over to him.

This supreme leadership role is highly unlikely, and it is not even certain that Inkpaduta participated in all four battles. Gary Clayton Anderson, a prominent Dakota historian, dismissed the claims that Inkpaduta was commander in chief of the Sioux forces. He noted, "There were many Sioux bands involved in these campaigns and there never was one man elected to run them. The Sioux people simply never operated that way." Chiefs led by personal influence and respect. There had been some powerful village leaders, but rarely did a chief garner such acclaim that he could influence a band — let alone control warriors from all three divisions of the Sioux.[49]

The official military records of the campaigns do not name Inkpaduta as the head military commander. Nor do the individual accounts kept by soldiers such as Isaac Heard, a Minnesotan who fought at Big Mound, Dead Buffalo Lake, and Stoney Lake, mention Inkpaduta in this capacity. Heard, in his memoirs of the campaign, *History of the Sioux War and the Massacres of 1862 and 1863*, never acknowledged Inkpaduta as a key leader of the Sioux.

Inkpaduta's age also suggests he was likely no longer a warrior leader by 1862. By this time, he was at least forty-eight years old, past the age of an active warrior. He would still have fought, probably in defensive actions to protect his village or people, but warrior chiefs were typically younger men in their twenties or thirties. Sitting Bull, a renowned warrior who likely did fight in the 1860s campaigns, was in his mid-forties at the Battle of the Little Big Horn. However, at this engagement in 1876 — the most famous battle with which he is associated — he, too, was no longer an active warrior or war leader and did not participate in the fighting.

We can ask how this image of Inkpaduta emerged. Partly, it

arose from the white view of an evil Inkpaduta who was capable of anything. Also following the death of Little Crow Inkpaduta was the Dakota leader most recognized by whites. Moreover, this image originated among the Dakotas. Once they had lost the war and wanted to make peace, they feared retribution for past acts. The Dakotas became quite adept at blaming raids, atrocities, and war leadership on Inkpaduta—a man the whites would readily accept in this villain role. William Folwell wrote, "The willingness of these [Dakota] witnesses to make Inkpaduta a scapegoat is clearly apparent."[50]

As the military campaign against the Dakotas commenced in late summer 1863, a large body of Sissetons and Wahpetons under Standing Buffalo, Scarlet Plume, and other chiefs was encamped east of the Missouri River near the tributaries of the James River. This was an area of many lakes and springs with fishing, buffalo, and good grass for the horses. On July 1 a buffalo hunt moved the villages southward to Big Mound in present-day North Dakota. It was here, three weeks later, that Inkpaduta and six lodges joined them. Inkpaduta camped with two other Santee resister bands led by Lean Bear and White Lodge.[51]

A short time after Inkpaduta's arrival in the camp, a hunter brought word of the approach of Sibley's column yelling, "All the Americans in the land are right here." Having received word from three buffalo hunters of the presence of a six-hundred-lodge village, Sibley's strike force pressed forward. The army's arrival at the camp on July 24 threw the village into a panic, with Standing Buffalo and Scarlet Plume ready to surrender. Joseph La Framboise, scouting for Sibley, rode out to the village and assured the Indians that Sibley was willing to talk. As a council was being planned, Tall Crown, a warrior said to be a follower of Inkpaduta, shot and killed Josiah Weiser, a doctor with the expedition. This attack caused the battle to commence around 5:00 P.M.[52]

The first casualties were the older warriors and chiefs who

went out to meet with Sibley; as they turned to flee, many were gunned down. The Dakotas fought well, charging to put the soldiers on the defensive then wheeling away as they fired a volley. But the warriors were not well armed. They were equipped mainly with shotguns, a few rifles, and bows, and they lacked ammunition. As the soldiers advanced, the Dakotas were forced to give ground, making one last stand at a slough at dusk. Defeated, the warriors were routed from the field, having protected their families long enough to escape.[53]

It was in defense of the village as part of the rearguard action that Inkpaduta fought and performed well. Inkpaduta's actions, however, did not stop many Dakotas from later blaming the battle on him. They accused him of killing the doctor, whether this account was accurate or not. Standing Bear's Sissetons left the camp and headed toward Canada. The next day, the remaining Dakotas encountered a large body of Lakotas, consisting of Hunkpapas and Blackfeet, who had crossed the Missouri to hunt buffalo. The Lakotas, still smarting from their loss in the First Sioux War and upset by the large numbers of miners passing through their lands en route to the mine fields of Montana, readily joined their brethren in two further battles against Sibley's troops.[54]

The battles at Dead Buffalo Lake on July 26 and Stoney Lake on July 28 inflicted further defeats on the Sioux. These battles were mainly large skirmishes, with the Sioux attempting to stop the soldiers' advance. The firepower and discipline of the army proved more than the Sioux could handle. Casualties on both sides were not heavy, with the Sioux claiming a loss of only twenty-four men killed. It is not clear if Inkpaduta took part in these later two battles; he may have left with the other Dakotas after Big Mound. Following these engagements, the Sioux retreated to the west bank of the Missouri River. After Sibley's army departed the area, the Yanktonais and Dakotas — and likely Inkpaduta — returned to the east side of the river in order to hunt buffalo.[55]

During the Sibley campaign, an atrocity occurred that shocked the soldiers; again it was blamed on Inkpaduta's band. Henson Wiseman was an enlisted soldier serving in Company I, Second Nebraska Cavalry, which was part of Sully's column. He had joined the army during the Dakota War in order to defend the frontier from Indian attack. His wife, Phoebe, and five of their children remained at the family farm near St. James, Nebraska. Henson had wanted his wife to move into town while he was away, but she refused, as she believed there was no danger of an Indian attack. On July 16, needing supplies, Phoebe walked the three and a half miles to St. James, leaving the children in the charge of Arthur, her sixteen-year-old son. She purchased some goods in St. James before taking the stagecoach to Elm Grove, where she spent the night with friends. The next day, Phoebe returned home to a horrible tragedy. Indians had attacked the farm killing three of her children and leaving the remaining two, Hannah and Loren, mortally wounded; both died within five days. Phoebe fled to St. James for help. Men returned with her to the farm but could do nothing. Two detachments of South Dakota cavalry tried to track the raiders but failed.[56]

Although the children did not live long enough to identify their attackers and the first newspaper accounts listed none of the culprits' names, an officer in an Iowa regiment was the first to accuse one of Inkpaduta's sons of the crime. In 1928 the South Dakota Historical Society stated in its collections that Inkpaduta's son — unnamed — had perpetrated the massacre. Robinson indicted Inkpaduta for the attack.[57] His name merely linked to that tragic event, Inkpaduta is often held responsible even though no eyewitness identified him or any member of his band. These claims stand as another example of the efforts to depict Inkpaduta as the mythic savage of white imagination.

It was also Robinson who argued that Inkpaduta was the leader of the Sioux at the Battle of Whitestone Hill. On September 3 a large camp of Hunkpapas, led by Black Moon; Yanktonais, with their chiefs Big Head and Two Bears; and smaller groups of Dakotas under White Lodge, Lean Bear, and Inkpaduta crossed back over the Missouri River. They were hunting buffalo when a detachment of Sully's column discovered them. Maj. Albert House and three hundred men of the Sixth Iowa Cavalry had stumbled upon the large encampment while out scouting for the Sioux. His forces outnumbered by at least three to one, House sent messengers back to Sully requesting immediate assistance. Actually, House was not in much danger; surprised by the army, the Sioux were preparing to escape and were not interested in a battle with their families so close by. Warriors bought time by taunting the soldiers as they encircled the troops' defensive position on a hill. Chiefs offered to talk with the soldiers in order to allow the women time to take down the lodges and collect supplies.[58]

One persistent myth of the ensuing battle is that knowing he had the soldiers trapped on the hill, Inkpaduta, the supposed leader of the Sioux, delayed the attack that would have annihilated the enemy in order to better prepare for combat. Robinson, Clodfelter, and Van Nuys all support this version of the battle, citing Inkpaduta's vanity as the reason for the Sioux loss. However, no white participant of the engagement claimed such hesitation by Inkpaduta occurred. In addition, the official reports of the action do not mention this delay by the Sioux to prepare for battle or that House's command was surrounded, soon to be overrun.[59] As has been stated, Inkpaduta was not the main leader of the village and did not have the authority or control over the warriors to implement such a delay.

This story probably stems from another version of the battle that had Inkpaduta taking a purification bath in a sweat lodge when the soldiers were first noticed. Neither account is factual, as Inkpaduta, out hunting, was not even present for the engagement. Inkpaduta had left one of his wives and two of his children in the village under the care of Medicine Bear, a Yanktonais leader, while he and his older sons went hunting for game. His family was present when Sully and the main force arrived and threatened to surround the large village. Fighting became general, with units of cavalry engaging the Sioux all over the field. The Sioux took heavy losses, trying to block the attacking soldiers from the noncombatants. To the Sioux, Whitestone Hill was not a battle, but a slaughter. Estimates of Sioux casualties range from 150 to 300 people (mainly women and children) killed and another 250 wounded or captured.[60]

Whitestone Hill was the final engagement of the 1863 campaign. The soldiers left for winter quarters, and the Sioux scattered into a number of villages and bands. Inkpaduta either moved toward the Minnesota border or remained along the James River throughout the winter and spring. Victor Renville, a mixed-blood son of a trader, wrote that one of Inkpaduta's grandsons was killed in the 1863 campaign.[61] If true, Inkpaduta's revenge raid at Spirit Lake had cost him great personal loss. Two sons, a nephew, and now a grandson had perished in the fighting since the massacre. Knowing the whites would never allow him to surrender and live in peace, Inkpaduta was forced to stay out of their reach by moving from the Dakotas to the Yanktons and then the Yanktonais. His kinship ties with all three groups would assist him in surviving. Inkpaduta had astutely married into all three bands. It is unclear how many wives Inkpaduta had over his lifetime, but family tradition states that when one wife died, Inkpaduta would quickly remarry. This would also explain his ability to keep fathering children well into his sixties. He cemented good relations with many bands through marriage. However, Inkpaduta was popular with the Sioux even where such kinship bonds did not exist. He was welcome in any village because of his reputation as a good man, a dependable warrior, and a patriot.[62] In 1864 the status of Inkpaduta would be challenged again as a new military campaign against the Sioux commenced.

## CHAPTER 7

# "The Incorrigible Hostile"

## LITTLE BIG HORN

The U.S. Army's 1864 campaign against the Sioux led to the Battle of Killdeer Mountain — the largest, in terms of numbers involved, Indian engagement in the history of the United States. Inkpaduta was again named, by white writers, the leader of the combined Sioux forces, as he would later be said to play a pivotal role in the most famous Indian battle in history, at Little Big Horn. In the years between the two engagements, Inkpaduta continued to elude all efforts to apprehend him. This only added to his status among whites as the premier Sioux enemy in the West.

Little Crow, Sitting Bull, and Crazy Horse all came under attack by whites for their warfare against American settlers and the military. They, too, were referred to as savages and dehumanized by whites fearful of these Indians' resistance to assimilation. But Little Crow was killed toward the end of the Dakota War of 1862, and Sitting Bull and Crazy Horse would both surrender to white authorities before they were murdered on the reservations. Ultimately, in the minds of whites, these warriors had succumbed to the superior culture and been "punished" for their crimes. They were no longer a threat and could, over time, be rehabilitated in white memory as worthy opponents who fought for the betterment of their people. Not so for Inkpaduta, the one Sioux leader who was never captured or punished for his crimes; he would die of natural causes in Canada. For this reason, Inkpaduta remained, for whites, a savage—untamed and irredeemable. The vilification of Inkpaduta would continue.

After the battles in 1863, Inkpaduta's band broke off from the other Sioux in order to replenish much-needed supplies lost in the fighting. While Inkpaduta hunted, his sons, including his second set of twins, Sounds The Ground As He Walks and Tracking White Earth, participated in a horse-stealing raid before returning to winter with their father among the Yanktonais.[1]

In June 1864 a two-pronged offensive commanded by General Sully moved west to confront the Sioux once again. This time the Lakotas—consisting mainly of the Blackfeet, Hunkpapas, Miniconjous, and San Arc bands—were heavily involved and ready for a fight. United with the Yanktonais and Dakotas, they felt strong enough to defeat the army. The desire for battle intensified when, on June 28, a cavalry patrol killed three warriors in an ambush. Sully ordered the dead Indians' heads to be cut off and mounted on poles. Shocked by this brutal act, the Sioux prepared for combat.[2]

Inkpaduta was not present as the campaign opened, but a messenger was sent to find him. The Lakotas thought highly of Inkpaduta and wanted him to join the alliance. When Inkpaduta and his band arrived, rather than camping with the other Dakotas or the Yanktonais, Inkpaduta set up his village next to the Lakotas, indicative of Inkpaduta's break with the Dakotas. He probably realized that both the Dakotas and the Yanktonais were prepared to make peace, which would leave him vulnerable to arrest or murder by the white authorities. Old Bull, a Lakota, remembered Inkpaduta joining the Hunkpapas in 1864; Inkpa-

Battle of Killdeer Mountain, July 28, 1864. During the battle, Inkpaduta led a desperate counter-attack to stop the advancing soldiers. Artist: Carl L. Boeckmann. Courtesy of the Minnesota Historical Society.

duta's cousin had married into that band, as had two of his daughters—one married End Of Horn, while another wedded Bull Ghost.[3] Once again, kinship ties would protect Inkpaduta's future.

On July 28 Sully and twenty-two hundred soldiers reached Killdeer Mountain. Here as many as sixteen hundred Lakotas—including Sitting Bull, Yanktonais, and Dakota warriors—waited for battle in front of their immense encampment. The Lakotas were flanked to one side; the Yanktonais and Dakotas, along with Inkpaduta and his men, were on the other. Both Robinson and Van Nuys claimed that the Lakotas had such a high opinion of Inkpaduta that they asked him to take command. As no such request would have been made—especially to such an elderly leader—Inkpaduta led only his own men and a few Yanktonais. Taking a position in a ravine, they planned to fight on foot. This was in contrast to the majority of the Sioux, who fought mounted.[4] Once more Inkpaduta was prepared to fight a defensive battle against the army in order to protect his people.

Having placed his units in a long, shallow, square formation, Sully started a slow, methodical advance toward the village. Resistance grew fiercer as the soldiers drew closer, but the Sioux were unable to pierce the square. As was the case in the battles of 1863, better firepower, including artillery, and unit discipline defeated the more poorly armed and independent-minded warriors. The Sioux had been so confident of victory that they had left the village lodges standing and encouraged the women and children to watch the battle. Now, as the battle turned against the Sioux, the noncombatants raced to pull down the lodges and escape.[5]

Late in the day, Inkpaduta led a charge out of the ravine in defense of the retreating villagers. Striking on Sully's right, Inkpaduta's men were counterattacked by a mounted charge of Minnesota cavalry armed with sabers. The Dakotas and Yanktonais held their ground in close hand-to-hand fighting before slowly withdrawing. The engagement continued over a mile and a half until the Sioux reached another ravine. Dismounting, the soldiers poured a heavy fire into the wooded ravine. Inkpaduta tried to launch a new attack, only to have well-placed artillery rounds cause his men finally to break and run.[6]

Routed from the field, the Sioux lost large quantities of lodges, food, and other supplies. The extent of casualties suffered was not heavy; the Sioux claimed they lost only 31 men killed while the army estimated 100 to 150 enemy dead. However, Killdeer Mountain was a devastating defeat in the amount of property lost by the Sioux.[7]

As the Sioux alliance broke up into smaller bands, Inkpaduta led his band to the Mouse River close to the Canadian border. They encamped near present-day Bismarck, North Dakota, in an area of deep ravines and canyons known as Dog's Den, which lay roughly forty miles from the Missouri River. He remained there for the rest of the summer.[8]

On August 30 Sully returned eastward at the end of his campaign. Passing by Fort Berthold, he learned of Inkpaduta's presence at Dog's Den. As a young officer at Fort Ridgely, Sully had participated in the army's efforts to find Inkpaduta in the 1850s. Still smarting from these failures, Sully jumped at the opportunity to finally corner Inkpaduta. Taking handpicked troops and traveling light, Sully marched on Dog's Den. Sully advanced sixty miles in two days and reached the area on September 1. The next day, he led his men on the attack, only to discover still-warm campfires but no people. Inkpaduta had narrowly escaped once again. Having eluded the soldiers, Inkpaduta may have headed into Canada to spend the winter at Turtle Mountain.[9]

By 1865 the Yanktonais and Dakotas had had enough of war. The Dakotas were destitute, and members either crossed over into Canada or surrendered to the army. In October the Yanktonais and Lakotas signed a treaty at Fort Sully agreeing to cease fighting.[10] Two years later, a treaty with the exiled or resister

Dakotas officially ended all warfare between them and the government. They received reservations in the Dakota Territory and at Fort Peck, Montana. Only Dakotas considered renegades such as Inkpaduta were not allowed to surrender. Abandoned in turn by the Dakotas, Yanktons, and Yanktonais, Inkpaduta had to move farther west to live among the Lakotas. Inkpaduta was becoming a living symbol of the decline of the great Sioux nation. The Dakotas, Yanktons, and Yanktonais had all been forced onto reservations, many only after fighting disastrous wars that failed to bring back their old independent lifestyles. Inkpaduta had been a witness to, and involved in, the downfall of all three groups. Only the Lakotas retained a certain degree of autonomy, which would soon be challenged by the encroaching whites. Attempting to avoid new conflicts with the whites — and fighting only to protect his freedom or defend noncombatants — Inkpaduta would play his part in the upcoming final encounters.

Details on the life of the elusive Inkpaduta from 1867 to 1875 become even more enigmatic. The last small bands of resister Dakotas merged together under Inkpaduta and other leaders such as Big Eagle, White Hat, and Standing Buffalo. Morale was low and a number of Dakotas including Big Eagle, eventually surrendered to the army. Only those such as Inkpaduta, for whom surrender was not an option, continued to head farther west. During the winter of 1867–68, Inkpaduta's band had a positive turn of fortune by joining Sitting Bull's village on the Missouri River. They found support and encouragement from the rising Lakota leader. Sitting Bull believed he had a kindred spirit in Inkpaduta, a man who kept to the old ways by refusing the reservation life and maintaining his independence. The Dakotas were soon assimilated into Sitting Bull's Hunkpapa band. The Hunkpapas thought highly of Inkpaduta, considering him a brave, courageous warrior and a hard worker who was kind to his family. At the same time, they pitied him for the hard life he had led since 1857, constantly pursued by the U.S. Army.[11]

For the remainder of the 1860s and through the early 1870s, Inkpaduta's band roamed along the Powder River or the region of the upper Missouri River. Inkpaduta was said to have fought and won a skirmish with the Crees, who were traditional enemies of the Lakotas. Meanwhile, his son Sounds The Ground As He Walks went raiding with Sitting Bull, running off horses at Fort Stevenson and attacking a wagon train close to Fort Totten.[12]

Rumors persisted of Inkpaduta's continued militarism during this period. Clodfelter related that Inkpaduta led raids back into Minnesota in 1865 and 1866. Robinson maintained that Inkpaduta not only took part in Red Cloud's War but also participated in the Fetterman Fight. Neither author provided sources regarding these claims.[13]

These rumors demonstrated the continuing fear of Inkpaduta as well as of his sons during this time, even in areas where Inkpaduta no longer traveled. For example, in Iowa Joseph Henry Taylor recalled meeting up with a mixed-blood while trapping in 1866. The mixed-blood asked if Taylor had seen anyone pass. After Taylor answered no, the man said he was lucky as "Inkpaduta's boys don't often let a chance slip." Taylor then scouted the area and found the tracks of six men. When he later heard of an attack near Peterson that left a soldier dead, Taylor was convinced it was the work of Inkpaduta's sons. "Striking the valley of the Little Sioux at least once a year on a hostile raid," wrote Taylor, "seemed to be a fanatical observance of Inkpaduta's band they could not abandon." To Taylor there could be no other American Indian responsible for the raid — only Inkpaduta.[14]

Another story illustrates how the image of Inkpaduta was transferred to all male members of his family. Those Dakotas who had neither participated in the Dakota War of 1862 nor surrendered soon after were removed from Minnesota and sent to the Crow Creek Reservation on the Missouri River. Here, large numbers of Sioux were soon joined by two thousand Ho-Chunks who also were banned from Minnesota although they took no part in the war. Reverend John Williamson, a missionary to the Dakotas, had voluntarily stayed with his flock when they were moved to the new reservation. In January 1864 the hungry Dakotas sent out a hunting party to find buffalo; Williamson went with them to ensure there would be no problems with whites. The hunting party of three hundred to four hundred Dakotas, one hundred Ho-Chunks, and four white men journeyed up the James River and then to the Minnesota border. In early February three un-known Dakota men approached the hunting party. Before greeting their visitors, the hunters hid the white men in a lodge. The men, who claimed to be out searching for horses, were invited to stay, but one of them, Hewanjiden, a grandson of Inkpaduta, was viewed with suspicion. Williamson, allowed out of the lodge, approached Hewanjiden. Fearing a trap, the Indian gave the missionary a "fierce glance of the incorrigible hostile," according to Williamson. After ten days, Hewanjiden, whom was Williamson called the "wild one," left the camp having taken with him two women, one married to a much older man.[15]

As Inkpaduta dwelled in the lands of the Lakotas, the federal government proceeded toward its goal of placing the last free Sioux onto a reservation. In 1868 various chiefs of the seven Lakota bands signed the Fort Laramie Treaty. This established the Great Sioux Reservation in the southwestern corner of the Dakota Territory. The reservation included the Black Hills, a region held sacred by the Sioux. Roughly half of the Lakotas moved onto the reservation, although many would leave in the summer months to return to the plains to hunt. The remainder of the Lakotas—led by chiefs such as Sitting Bull, Crazy Horse, and Gall—refused to recognize the treaty or set foot on the reservation. To the government these Sioux became "hostiles" unwilling to abandon their traditional way of life.

In 1875 a showdown occurred when gold was discovered in the Black Hills. The small regular army contingent made a futile effort to keep the large numbers of miners from entering the reservation, and the government ultimately decided it would be simpler to buy the area from the Sioux. The attempt to purchase the Black Hills met with an adamant refusal on the part of the Lakotas. The government quickly blamed this reluctance to sell on the "hostile" Lakotas who did not live on the reservation. Defeat them, it was reasoned, and a new treaty could be worked out. In early 1876 the army was given the task of conquering the Lakota holdouts.

The Great Sioux War opened with an inconclusive winter campaign. The army then prepared a three-pronged summer campaign to defeat the Sioux and their allies, the Northern Cheyennes. The military was working under two wrong assumptions: that the hostiles were not numerous, and that upon contact they would scatter into small bands. Both views proved disastrously wrong. Inspired by leaders such as Sitting Bull and seeing the upcoming war as a fight for national survival as a free people, thousands of Sioux left the reservations to join the hostile bands. An immense village of some six thousand to seven thousand people with fifteen hundred warriors roamed through northern Wyoming and southern Montana. In addition, the Sioux and Northern Cheyennes did not intend to shy away from battle.

General George Crook and his column advancing northward from Wyoming were the first to encounter this firm resistance. On June 17, at the Battle of the Rosebud, Crook's command was attacked by Crazy Horse and other chiefs leading their men in an amazingly well coordinated assault. After a hard fight, Crook was able to fend off the Sioux and Cheyennes but then withdrew from the field to regroup. The day's success raised the morale of the resisters, as did a vision by Sitting Bull that another defeat of the army was imminent. Inkpaduta was present in the camp for this proclamation of victory.

In 1871 Gen. D.S. Stanley submitted to the War Department a report on the number of nonreservation Sioux under Sitting

Bull. The report stated three small Santee bands, one of them
Inkpaduta's, and a few Yanktonais were with the charismatic
leader. But some time after this, Inkpaduta led his people into
Canada. Life was not easy there, and perhaps as early as the fall
of 1875, Inkpaduta once more journeyed into the United States.
He Dog, a Lakota who knew Inkpaduta well, said he returned
solely to hunt buffalo for his hungry people; he was not intending to make war. This view is collaborated by Wooden Leg, a
Northern Cheyenne. Wooden Leg remembered the appearance
of Inkpaduta's band as it arrived at the resisters' camp in late
April. The people had little property, few guns, and dogs had to
drag the lodges from a lack of horses. The "no clothing people"
was what the other Sioux and Cheyennes called them.[16] Caught
up in the midst of a new war, Inkpaduta's small band was safest
with the resister camp.

The size and makeup of Inkpaduta's village has been debated.
There were two Dakota bands in the village — Inkpaduta's num-
bering fifteen lodges, and White Eagle's consisting of fifteen to
twenty lodges. Together, an estimated thirty to forty Santee
lodges were present. The bands consisted of Mdewakantons, Sissetons, and Wahpekutes. Nicholas Ruleau, a French fur trader
who had dealings with the Lakotas, claimed that the two Dakota
bands could field eighty warriors for combat.[17] Also debated
was the location of the Santee bands inside the larger Lakota
encampment.

Red Horse, a Miniconjou chieftain, placed the Dakotas at the
top or northern end of the combined village; however, it is more
likely they encamped at the southern end. Both Gall and Crazy
Horse stated that the Dakotas were at the southern end of the
encampment.[18] They were dwelling on the Little Big Horn River
when Lt. Col. George Armstrong Custer attacked the village on
June 25.

Custer and roughly six hundred men of the Seventh Cavalry
made up the second prong of the army's offensive. Custer was to

strike the hostiles and drive them up the Little Big Horn — into the arms of the third prong under Gen. Alfred Terry if all went as planned. Custer pushed his march hard, arriving in the Little Big Horn valley on the 25th. This was a day earlier than Terry could get into position to block the Sioux to the north. Initially planning to rest a day, Custer changed his mind when he believed the Seventh had been sighted by the Sioux. Without reconnoitering, Custer divided his command into four detachments. Capt. Frederick Benteen and three companies were sent off to the lower end of the valley to ensure the Sioux did not flee to the south, away from Terry's forces to the north. Another company was left to protect the slow-moving supply train. With three companies, Maj. Marcus Reno was ordered to attack the lower end of the village while Custer promised to support him with the remaining five companies. Custer intended to strike farther upstream, dividing the defenders and causing confusion.

There is wide variance in Sioux recollections over Inkpaduta's role in the Battle of the Little Big Horn. Some accounts contend that the nearly blind chief, at least sixty-one years old, but possibly older, was fishing with his grandsons when Reno's assault began on the lower end of the village. Inkpaduta was led away from the fighting by his grandsons and took no part in the battle. Ambrose Little Ghost relates that Inkpaduta put Little Ghost, Inkpaduta's four-year-old son (and Ambrose Little Ghost's grandfather), on a horse behind a tribal elder and led him safely from the village.[19]

Other Sioux recollections place Inkpaduta in the thick of the fighting. Eastman heard that Inkpaduta was "a great factor in the Custer battle," and Waggoner believed Inkpaduta fought against Custer — not Reno. In 1896 Gall, one of the main Lakota leaders at the battle, told Robinson and others that Inkpaduta commanded the fight against Reno. As ordered by Custer, Reno charged the village, but the major hesitated when he encountered the immense size of the camp and dismounted his men. Under heavy pressure by large numbers of warriors, Reno first

retreated to some trees along the Little Big Horn before divert-
ing his troops to a line of bluffs across the river. Shaken and in a
near panic, Reno held out at this location, joined by Benteen's
detachment and the supply train. Gall claimed that when the
soldiers fled the trees, he told Inkpaduta to keep Reno retreating and left him in charge as he led his men against Custer.[20]

Relying on Gall's statement, Van Nuys went so far as to make
Inkpaduta the architect of Custer's defeat, who shrewdly under-
stood the flow of the battle and led the Sioux to victory.[21] Yet,
there are several reasons to question Inkpaduta's supposed combat role. It is extremely doubtful that at his age, Inkpaduta
would have been considered a war leader or would even have
fought in the engagement. By comparison, Crazy Horse and
Gall, two of the main Lakota leaders at the battle, were both in
their thirties. Nor would a half-blind Inkpaduta have been called
upon to lead a major portion of the fighting, even if the Sioux
actually had that sort of combat chain of command. Lastly, Gall's
first account of the battle, coming soon after the engagement,
did not mention Inkpaduta or name him as a prominent leader.
With or without Inkpaduta's aid, the Sioux won a major victory
over the U.S. Army at the Little Big Horn.

The Battle of the Little Big Horn and the death of Custer, a
Civil War hero, were shocking blows to the American nation.
Many Sioux and Northern Cheyennes feared retribution for
their part in the fight. Thus, when interviewed by whites about
the engagement, they were not always truthful in their answers;
often they played the old game of blaming Inkpaduta. Others
merely told white interviewers what they wanted to hear. As
Robinson had already depicted Inkpaduta as a savage, it was
likely that Gall related the story Robinson craved: a militaristic
Inkpaduta making war against the whites nearly twenty years
after the Spirit Lake massacre. Casting Inkpaduta as the main
leader also conveniently shifted attention away from other, responsible chiefs.

A more intriguing story in regard to the battle involves Inkpaduta's twin sons Sounds The Ground As He Walks and Tracking White Earth. There is no doubt they took part in the battle, fighting against Custer's column. After seeing Reno in the trees along the river, Custer assumed Reno was in a good defensive position. As Reno's men occupied the attention of the defenders of the village, Custer decided to head up the river to attack the camp at its northern end. Custer soon realized the vast size of the village and sent for help from Benteen. In the controversial fight that followed, Custer and his force were caught between the forces of Gall and Crazy Horse and were wiped out. Sounds The Ground As He Walks reportedly killed Custer. For his part, Tracking White Earth was mortally wounded during the fighting.

Following the battle, there was a fascination among whites to determine which warrior actually killed Custer. Many names have been mentioned, including Rain in the Face and Wooden Leg. But many Sioux claimed it was Sounds The Ground As He Walks. Red Horse believed that a Dakota killed Custer and took his horse, and that Inkpaduta's sons shot the last soldier on Custer's Hill who tried to escape toward the river. After the battle, White Bull, Sitting Bull's nephew, encountered Sounds The Ground As He Walks leading Custer's horse. "Is that a good horse?" asked White Bull. "I know it is a good horse as it was Long Hair's [Custer's]," responded Sounds The Ground As He Walks. Iron Hail was another Lakota who saw Inkpaduta's son with Custer's horse. Eastman, who was not present at the battle, remembered Lakota warriors telling him that a son of Inkpaduta killed Custer.[22]

There is no definitive way to know who killed Custer or when he died during the battle. It is possible that Sounds The Ground As He Walks simply ended up with Custer's horse. Again, crediting Sounds The Ground As He Walks with killing Custer could be another case of the Sioux either telling the whites what they wanted to hear or shifting blame onto Inkpaduta's family to avoid possible punishment. What is known is that Inkpaduta suffered yet another personal loss — the death of another son — at the Little Big Horn.

After keeping the battered remains of the Seventh Cavalry besieged on Reno's Hill for another day, the Sioux struck camp and moved south, away from Terry's approaching army. It had been a great victory as predicted by Sitting Bull; finding some whiskey, members of Inkpaduta's village celebrated by getting drunk and firing their guns into the air. But the battle also meant the doom of the Lakotas. Outraged by the loss of Custer, many Americans demanded revenge against the Sioux. Sitting Bull, seen as the man primarily responsible for the defeat, replaced Inkpaduta as the principal enemy among the Sioux. The *New York Herald* denounced him saying, "Everything that is cruel and vicious is a matter of ostentation and pride to him."[23]

Large military reinforcements were sent to the area while the resisters, unable to feed such a large village, broke into smaller camps as winter approached. The army pursued a winter campaign that broke the resisting bands' will to continue the war. Never safe from attack, unable to hunt in peace, villages started to surrender; by the summer of 1877, even Crazy Horse gave up. Only Sitting Bull refused to surrender. He went into exile, crossing the border into Canada.

During that summer Inkpaduta and Long Dog, a Hunkpapa chief, broke off from Sitting Bull's camp. They took their combined thirty lodges across the Missouri River to Wolf's Point near a subagency of the Fort Peck Reservation in Montana. On September 9 Terry received word of their presence. He sent Major Reno to attack the renegades. Arriving on September 13, Reno found no sign of Sioux but learned they had crossed into Canada.[24] Old and nearly blind, Inkpaduta still eluded the army's efforts to corner him.

Sometime before entering Canada, Inkpaduta rejoined Sitting Bull and settled alongside other Wahpekutes living in Can-

ada on the Oak Lake Reserve near Brandon, Manitoba. Local
Sissetons, who were dwelling close by at Wood Mountain, wanted
nothing to do with Inkpaduta. They feared he would bring trouble from the Canadian government. Knowing that many Dakotas
still blamed him for the deaths of their loved ones in the Dakota War, Inkpaduta lived in isolation afraid he would be murdered. He attempted to reestablish kinship bonds with relatives,
hunted, and became a farmer. As was ever his practice as he
roamed the West, he started a garden. In 1877 the Canadian
government created a new reserve at Turtle Mountain for the
Wahpekutes. Here among his own band, Inkpaduta felt more
secure. In 1878 Inkpaduta fathered his final child, a daughter
named Oyate-Mani-Win. Inkpaduta could now grow old still surrounded by his young children — Charley Maku, Little Ghost,
and Oyate-Mani-Win.[25]

As with his birth, it is not certain when Inkpaduta died. Most
sources indicate his death occurred in 1879. Waggoner, Eastman,
and a Father Laviolette, a Catholic priest caring for the Canadian
Sioux, all reported that as the correct year of his death. While
out hunting, Inkpaduta allegedly caught pneumonia and soon
passed away. Waggoner heard the death occurred in June on
Berry Creek at the Pinpot Reserve in Saskatchewan.[26]

Little Ghost and Charley Maku, as well as Inkpaduta's daughter Oyate-Mani-Win, were with him when he died. Waggoner
reported these two sons were still alive in 1934, although an
older daughter of Inkpaduta had died in 1924. One of the sons
became a Christian, and both were farmers. In 1944, while doing
research for a book on the Sioux in Canada, Father Laviolette
also spoke with the sons, who were old men by that time. Other
relatives and descendants of Inkpaduta continued to live in Canada and throughout the northern plains.[27]

Occasionally members of Inkpaduta's family still could cause
a stir. In 1881 Philip Wells was serving as an interpreter at Fort
Buford in Montana. Hungry and homesick, Sitting Bull and his

people returned to the United States and surrendered at the fort. Wells remembered a young man, weak from hunger and very ill, who was placed in the post hospital. Over time, Wells came to know this young man quite well. He said he was a grandson of Inkpaduta. His father (perhaps Tracking White Earth) had died five years earlier in 1876. Lying to protect his family and band, he claimed he was the last living member of Inkpaduta's band. He never recovered from his hardships. This lingering fear of punishment for being related to Inkpaduta was commonly felt among family members. One of Inkpaduta's daughters never spoke of her father for this reason.[28] Even after the death of Inkpaduta, the U.S. government still had concerns over the possible threat of Inkpaduta's band.

During the Ghost Dance crisis in 1890, Gen. Nelson Miles claimed that Sitting Bull had sent word to all the bands of the Sioux. This included Inkpaduta's band in Canada. Sitting Bull allegedly asked them to join him once more in resisting the whites. Although Sitting Bull did not in fact take this course of action, it would have been no help to him if he had. By the 1890s the remnants of Inkpaduta's band were living in misery in Canada, struggling to feed themselves and in no condition to make war on anyone.[29]

Inkpaduta died unpunished by the whites. He had escaped their efforts to apprehend him time and again, finally dying in a foreign country. By contrast, Little Crow, Crazy Horse, and Sitting Bull all were killed by whites or their American Indian supporters, and thus their images could be reconsidered after their deaths. They had paid the price for their supposed savageness and now could be found acceptable to whites. But Inkpaduta could never be redeemed or assimilated. He remained unpunished for his defiance of the United States and the massacre he committed at Spirit Lake.

By his ability to survive, Inkpaduta remains in white historical memory a savage. Even in the twenty-first century, the idea of the savage persists in some white writers' and historians' depictions of certain American Indians, such as Inkpaduta. Over a century and a half, Inkpaduta has been accused of such heinous crimes that his life has become a caricature of evil on the level of a comicbook villain, void of any decent values or virtues.

This perception by whites can be felt in more recent times. In his youth, a great-grandson of Inkpaduta pulled a prank that got him in some trouble. He was ordered to see a court-appointed psychologist. When the psychologist discovered the boy was a descendant of Inkpaduta, the doctor wrote in his report that the youth's actions were hereditary, caused by the evil nature of his ancestor, Inkpaduta.[30]

But to the Lakotas and Dakotas, Inkpaduta is a hero. He is a patriotic figure to be honored and revered. At Sioux gatherings, honor songs are sung about him and his role in defending his people. When four Dakota men entered the United States Army and prepared to fight in the Iraq War, they chose the symbolic warrior name Inkpaduta.[31]

Inkpaduta's life is symbolic of the final decline and fall of the great Sioux nation. His life's journey led him from the traditional society of the eastern Dakotas and their futile resistance in the Dakota War of 1862, through the treaties and military defeats of the Nakotas, and then to the last great victories and defeats of the Lakotas in the Sioux War of 1876. Along the way, Inkpaduta interacted with some of the legendary Sioux leaders and was himself greatly respected by them.

Inkpaduta's life was marked by his strong objection to white encroachment and his fierce desire to retain the traditional life of the Wahpekutes. He was not a perfect man, by any means, and his temper and frustrations with the changing times led him into conflict with incoming white settlers. Eventually, events beyond his control brought him to Spirit Lake and infamy. Yet, Inkpaduta was not an evil or violent man, nor a hater of whites. A large portion of his life was lived peacefully alongside white settlers.

After Spirit Lake, there is no evidence that Inkpaduta took any further offensive actions against the whites, fighting only when necessary to protect himself or his people.

Few men's lives have been so wrongly interpreted by history as that of Inkpaduta. Much of what whites have written about this Dakota leader is false and pure fantasy, at times reinforced by confusing testimony from some Sioux. The positive Dakota image of Inkpaduta has been overlooked. But this positive view of Inkpaduta must be included in any interpretation of his life. It is time to put the bias and bigotry of earlier eras behind us and to embrace a new approach in evaluating Inkpaduta's role in history — one that does not deny the events of the Spirit Lake massacre but moves to redeem Inkpaduta for white Americans.

# *Notes*

## INTRODUCTION

1. *St. Peter Courier*, May 20, 1857; Charles Flandrau, "The Ink-Pa-Du-Ta Massacre of 1857," in *Collections of the Minnesota Historical Society* (St. Paul: Minnesota Historical Society, 1880), 3:407; L.P. Lee, *History of the Spirit Lake Massacre* (Iowa City: State Historical Society of Iowa, 1918), 65–66.

2. Doane Robinson, *History of the Dakota or Sioux Indians* (Minneapolis: Ross and Haines, 1956), 342; Doane Robinson Papers, South Dakota Historical Society, Manuscript Collection, 1–2.

3. Robinson, *History of the Dakota*, 216, 344, 346, 360; Doane Robinson Papers, 10.

4. Michael Clodfelter, *The Dakota War: The United States Army versus the Sioux, 1862–1865* (Jefferson, N.C.: McFarland and Company, 1998), 23–25.

5. Maxwell Van Nuys, *Inkpaduta — the Scarlet Point: Terror of the Dakota Frontier and Secret Hero of the Sioux* (N.p.: privately published, 1998), i, 398–99.

## CHAPTER 1

1. Clair Jacobson, "A History of the Yanktonai and Hunkpatina Sioux," *North Dakota History* 47, no. 1 (Winter 1980): 4; Stephen E. Feraca and James H. Howard, "The Identity and Demography of the Dakota or Sioux Tribe," *Plains Anthropologist* (May 8–20, 1963), n.p.

2. Roy Meyer, *History of the Santee Sioux* (Lincoln: University of Nebraska Press, 1984), 13–14; Theodore C. Blegen, *Minnesota: A History of the State* (St. Paul: University of Minnesota Press, 1963), 216; John S. Wozniak, *Contact, Negotiation, and Conflict: An Ethnohistory of the Eastern Dakota, 1819–1839* (Washington, D.C.: University Press of America, 1978), 7; Guy Gibbon, *The Sioux: The Dakota and Lakota Nations* (Oxford: Blackwell Publishing, 2003), 52.

3. Gibbon, *The Sioux*, 51–52; Alan Woolworth and Nancy Woolworth, "Eastern Dakota Settlement and Subsistence Patterns Prior to 1851," *Minnesota Archaeologist* 39, no. 2, (May 1980): 80; Feraca and Howard, "Identity and Demography of the Dakota."

4. Richard White, "The Winning of the West: The Expansion of the Western Sioux in the Eighteenth Century," in *Major Problems in American Indian History*, ed. Albert Hurtado and Peter Iverson (Lexington, Mass.: D.C. Heath and Company, 1994), 247; Herbert T. Hoover, *The Yankton Sioux* (New York: Chelsea House Publications, 1988), 15.

5. Ruth Landes, *Mystic Lake Sioux: Sociology of the Mdewakantonwan Santee* (Madison: University of Wisconsin Press, 1968), 4; Samuel Pond, *The Dakota or Sioux in Minnesota, as They Were in 1834* (St. Paul: Minnesota Historical Society Press, 1986), 5; Woolworth and Woolworth, "Eastern Dakota Settlement," 72; Gibbon, *The Sioux*, 79.

6. Lucius Hubbard and Return Holcombe, *Minnesota in Three Centuries, 1655–1908* (Mankato: Publishing Society of Minnesota, 1908) 3:219; Louis H. Roddis, *The Indian Wars of Minnesota* (Cedar Rapids, Iowa: Torch Press, 1956), 22; Lee, *History of the Spirit Lake Massacre*, 69.

7. Doane Robinson Papers.

8. Mark Diedrich, *Famous Chiefs of the Eastern Sioux* (Minneapolis: Coyote Books, 1987), 43; Doane Robinson Papers; Frank Herriot Papers, Manuscript Collection, Minnesota Historical Society (hereafter cited as FHP).

9. Diedrich, *Famous Chiefs*, 43; E. H. Allison, "Sioux Proper Names," *South Dakota Historical Collections* (Pierre, S.D.: State Historical Society, 1912), 6:277; Doane Robinson Papers; Stephen R. Riggs, *Tah-Koo Wah-Kan; or, The Gospel among the Dakotas* (New York: Arno Press, 1972), 263;

Wozniak, *Contact, Negotiation, and Conflict*, 19; Pond, *The Dakota*, 146; Michael Clodfelter, *Dakota War,* 23; Roddis, *Indian Wars*, 22.

10. Charles Eastman, *Indian Boyhood* (New York: McClure and Phillips, 1902), 10–11, 49–50, 52, 57–58, 63; Pond, *The Dakota*, 142, 145; Wozniak, *Contact, Negotiation, and Conflict*, 19–20.

11. Eastman, *Indian Boyhood*, 18, 30, 64.

12. Landes, *Mystic Lake Sioux*, 96, 113; Wozniak, *Contact, Negotiation, and Conflict*, 6, 13; Gary Clayton Anderson, *Kinsmen of Another Kind: Dakota–White Relations in the Upper Mississippi Valley, 1650–1862* (Lincoln: University of Nebraska Press, 1984), 10, 58, 79.

13. Wozniak, *Contact, Negotiation, and Conflict*, 6, 16, 17–18; Landes, *Mystic Lake Sioux*, 14, 29, 31, 33–34, 37, 39, 45–46; Pond, *The Dakota*, 139.

14. Pond, *The Dakota*, 7, 66–67; Wozniak, *Contact, Negotiation, and Conflict*, 24; Landes, *Mystic Lake Sioux*, 78; Amos E. Oneroad, Alanson B. Skinner, Laura Anderson, eds., *Being Dakota: Tales and Traditions of the Sisseton and Wahpeton* (St. Paul: Minnesota Historical Society Press, 2003), 64.

15. Pond, *The Dakota*, 6, 68; Ruth Landes, "Dakota Warfare," *Southwestern Journal of Anthropology* 15 (1959): 47–48; Landes, *Mystic Lake Sioux*, 65.

16. Eastman, *Indian Boyhood*, 29; Pond, *The Dakota*, 26–27, 29; Woolworth and Woolworth, "Eastern Dakota Settlement," 72, 76, 78; Gibbon, *The Sioux*, 54; Anderson, *Kinsmen of Another Kind*, 3, 7; Blegen, *Minnesota*, 23.

17. Robinson, *History of the Dakota*, 255; Meyer, *History of the Santee Sioux*, 21–22; Roddis, *Indian Wars*, 9; Landes, *Mystic Lake Sioux*, 3; Woolworth and Woolworth, "Eastern Dakota Settlement," 86.

18. Annuity Payrolls for the Mdewakanton, Sisseton, and Wahpeton Sioux Tribes, 1853, Records of the Bureau of Indian Affairs, National Archives (NA) Record Group (RG) 75; Meyer, *History of the Santee Sioux*, 46; Gibbon, *The Sioux*, 79.

19. Thomas Hughes, *Indian Chiefs of Southern Minnesota* (Minneapolis: Ross and Haines, 1969), 7; Roddis, *Indian Wars*, 2; *Statistical Report on the Sickness and Mortality in the Army of the United States*, U.S. Army Surgeon-General's Office (Washington, D.C.: A.O.P. Nicholson Printers, 1856), 2:66.

20. Jacobson, "Yanktonai and Hunkpatina Sioux," 5, 8, 9; Blegen, *Minnesota*, 31, 65, 74; Gibbon, *The Sioux*, 48; Meyer, *History of the Santee Sioux*, 20.

21. Howard Paulson, "Federal Indian Policy and the Dakota Indians," *South Dakota History* 3, no. 3 (Summer 1973): 286, 291–93; Anderson, *Kinsmen of Another Kind*, 78; Elliot Coues, ed., *The Expeditions of Zebulon Montgomery Pike* (New York: Francis P. Harper, 1895), 1:43–48, 66–68; Robinson, *History of the Dakota*, 76–77.

22. Pond, *The Dakota*, 60–61; Roddis, *Indian Wars*, 14; Anderson, *Kinsmen of Another Kind*, 100.

23. Thomas L. McKenny to Superintendent of Indian Affairs William Clark, July 22, 1825, NA RG 75, Letters Sent (LS), Office of Indian Affairs; Agent Lawrence Taliaferro to Commissioner of Indian Affairs T.Hartley Crawford, September 30, 1839, NA RG 75, LS, St. Peter Agency; William H. Keating, *Narrative of an Expedition to the Source of St. Peter's River* (Minneapolis: Ross and Haines, 1959), 302–303; Anderson, *Kinsmen of Another Kind*, xvii, 107, 130.

24. Pond, *The Dakota*, 8; Wozniak, *Contact, Negotiation, and Conflict*, 9.

25. Landes, *Mystic Lake Sioux*, 38; Landes, "Dakota Warfare," 45.

26. Pond, *The Dakota*, 65, 121; Landes, "Dakota Warfare," 50.

27. Woolworth and Woolworth, "Eastern Dakota Settlement," 75; Pond, *The Dakota*, 60; Robinson, *History of the Dakota*, 67.

28. Nancy Bonvillain, *The Sac and Fox* (New York: Chelsea House Publishers, 1995), 42–43.

## CHAPTER 2

1. Hubbard and Holcombe, *Minnesota in Three Centuries*, 3:220–21; Robinson, *History of the Dakota*, 343; *Minnesota Pioneer and Democrat*, April 21, 1857; Joseph Henry Taylor, "Inkpaduta and Sons," *North Dakota Historical Quarterly* 4, no. 3 (October 1929–July 1930): 154; Lee, *Spirit Lake Massacre*, 66.

2. Robinson, *History of the Dakota*, 343; Clodfelter, *Dakota War*, 24; Doane Robinson Papers, 2–3; Landes, *Mystic Lake Sioux*, 91.

3. Clodfelter, *Dakota War*, 24; D. E. Clark, "The Spirit Lake Massacre," in *Iowa and War*, ed. BenjaminF. Shambaugh (Iowa City: State Historical Society of Iowa, 1917–19), no. 11, p. 5; Lee, *Spirit Lake Massacre*, 67.

4. Robinson, *History of the Dakota*, 342–43; Frank Herriot, "The Origins of the Indian Massacre between the Okobojis," *Annals of Iowa* 18 (1932): 357; Clodfelter, *Dakota War*, 23–24.

5. Peggy Larson, "Inkpaduta, Renegade Sioux" (Master's thesis,

Mankato State University, December 1969, at Iowa State Historical Library), 2–3; Herriot, "Indian Massacre," 356, Peggy Rodina Larson, "A New Look at the Elusive Inkpaduta," *Minnesota History* 48, no. 1 (Spring 1982): 25.

6. Anderson, *Kinsmen of Another Kind*, 80.

7. Doane Robinson Papers; Diedrich, *Famous Chiefs*, 43–44; Hoover, *Yankton Sioux*, 14; Wozniak, *Contact, Negotiation, and Conflict*, 2; Landes, "Dakota Warfare," 44; Landes, *Mystic Lake Sioux*, 26; letter, Alexander Ramsey to Commissioner of Indian Affairs, October 17, 1849, Senate Executive Document (SED) no. 5, 31st Cong., 1st sess., Series 550, 1018–19.

8. Anderson, *Kinsmen of Another Kind*, 73–74; Larson, "New Look," 26; William Watts Folwell, *A History of Minnesota* (St. Paul: Minnesota Historical Society Press, 1961), 2:400.

9. Diedrich, *Famous Chiefs*, 44.

10. Stephen R. Riggs, "Dakota Portraits," *Minnesota History Bulletin* 1 (1915): 500–502; Lucy Leavenworth Wilder Morris, ed., *Old Rail Fence Corners: Frontier Tales Told by Minnesota Pioneers* (St. Paul: Minnesota Historical Society Press, 1976), 80; author's interview with Ambrose Little Ghost, May 2, 2007.

11. Lawrence Taliaferro Papers, Journal, August 2 and 29, 1823, Manuscript Collection, Minnesota Historical Society (hereafter cited as LTP).

12. Council Notes from Prairie du Chien, August 8–10, 1825, William Clark Papers, Kansas State Historical Society (hereafter cited as WCP); LTP, June 22, 1833; Larson, "Inkpaduta, Renegade Sioux," 4; Joseph Frazier Wall, *Iowa: A Bicentennial History* (New York: W. W. Norton, 1978), 6–7.

13. LTP, February 20, March 21, December 28, 1828; Diedrich, *Famous Chiefs*, 44.

14. Diedrich, *Famous Chiefs*, 44.

15. Ibid., 46; LTP, December 28, 1828, January 12, July 4, 1829; William Clark to Secretary of War John Eaton, May 17, 1830, WCP, 4:113.

16. LTP, April 23, 1828, January 11 and 12, June 1, 1829; Taliaferro to William Clark, August 12, 1831, WCP, 6:287; Larson, "New Look," 26.

17. LTP, December 30, 1828, May 6, July 4, 1829; Ramsey to Commissioner of Indian Affairs, October 17, 1849, 1018–19.

18. LTP, March 29, April 1, 1829; Anderson, *Kinsmen of Another Kind*, 133.

19. Diedrich, *Famous Chiefs*, 44–45.

20. LTP, September 8, 1829.

21. William Clark to President Andrew Jackson, July 21, 1830, WCP, 4:139; Paulson, "Federal Indian Policy," 304–305, 307; Larson, "Inkpaduta, Renegade Sioux," 5; Wall, *Iowa*, 7–8.

22. LTP, August 19, 1830.

23. Diedrich, *Famous Chiefs*, 45; Larson, "Inkpaduta, Renegade Sioux," 6–7; Wall, *Iowa*, 12–13.

24. Larson, "New Look," 26; Diedrich, *Famous Chiefs*, 45, 47; Robinson, *History of the Dakota*, 165.

25. Lee, *Spirit Lake Massacre*, 65; Larson, "New Look," 26; Riggs, "Dakota Portraits," 500; Hubbard and Holcombe, *Minnesota in Three Centuries*, 3:219–20.

26. LTP, April 29, September 30, 1839; Taliaferro to Clark, August 8, 1831, WCP, 6:286; Diedrich, *Famous Chiefs*, 45.

27. Anderson, *Kinsmen of Another Kind*, 82; Diedrich, *Famous Chiefs*, 46.

28. Taliaferro to Crawford, September 30, 1839, NA RG 75, LS, St. Peter Agency; Diedrich, *Famous Chiefs*, 46; LTP, June 3, 1839.

29. Larson, "Inkpaduta, Renegade Sioux," 8; Diedrich, *Famous Chiefs*, 44, 46; Rhoda R. Gilman, *Henry Hastings Sibley: Divided Heart* (St. Paul: Minnesota Historical Society, 2004), 80–81; Flandrau, "Ink-Pa-Du-Ta Massacre of 1857," 3:387; Gibbon, *The Sioux*, 86; Robinson, *History of the Dakota*, 215.

30. Roddis, *Indian Wars*, 22; Diedrich, *Famous Chiefs*, 46; Larson, "New Look," 26.

31. Thomas Hughes, "Causes and Results of the Inkpaduta Massacre," *Collections of the Minnesota Historical Society* (1912), 14:264; Agnes C. Laut, "Pioneer Women of the West: The Heroines of Spirit Lake, Iowa," *The Outing* 51 (March 1908): 687–88.

32. Van Nuys, *Inkpaduta*, 3–4.

33. Doane Robinson Papers.

34. Clark, "Spirit Lake Massacre," 6; Bob Brown, "The Spirit Lake Massacre" (from *Fort Dodge Messenger*, February 18–23, 1957), 3; Larson, "New Look," 27; Diedrich, *Famous Chiefs*, 45; Hubbard and Holcombe, *Minnesota in Three Centuries*, 3:249; Taylor, "Inkpaduta and Sons," 154; Philip F. Wells to Frank Herriot, January 4, 1933, FHP; Herriot, "Indian Massacre," 380; Mary Hawler Bakeman, comp. and ed., *Legends, Letters, and Lies: Readings on the Spirit Lake Massacre of 1857* (Roseville, Minn.: Park Genealogical Boxes, 2001), 14.

35. Clark, "Spirit Lake Massacre," 6; Herriot, "Indian Massacre," 380; Larson, "New Look," 27; Joseph Henry Taylor, *Twenty Years on the Trap Line* (Bismarck, N.D., 1891), 14.

36. J. Waggoner to Frank Herriot, August 5, 1933, FHP; Larson, "Inkpaduta, Renegade Sioux," 20; author's interview with Danny Seaboy, May 29, 2007; interview with Little Ghost; Diedrich, *Famous Chiefs*, 45, 46, 48–49; Vernon Blank, "Inkpaduatah's Great White Friend," *Iowa Magazine* (December–January, 1960–61), 17; Larson, "New Look," 27.

37. J. Waggoner to Herriot, February 27, 1932, August 30, September 5, 1933, February 3, 1934, FHP; interview with Little Ghost; James H. Howard, *The Canadian Sioux* (Lincoln: University of Nebraska Press, 1984), 44–45.

38. Diedrich, *Famous Chiefs*, 46; Blank, "Inkpaduatah's Great White Friend," 17.

39. Herriot to Waggoner, April 11, 1934, FHP; author's interview with Ladonna Brave Bull Allard, April 24, 2007; Larson, "New Look," 35; Bakeman, *Legends, Letters, and Lies*, 14; Diedrich, *Famous Chiefs*, 45, 46; interview with Little Ghost; interview with Seaboy.

40. Riggs, "Dakota Portraits," 500.

41. Ramsey to Commissioner of Indian Affairs, October 17, 1849, 1019; Doane Robinson Papers; Robinson, *History of the Dakota*, 343; Waggoner to Herriot, November 30, 1932, FHP; Clodfelter, *Dakota War*, 24.

42. Larson, "New Look," 26–27; Alexander Ramsey to Luke Lea, Commissioner of Indian Affairs, September 23, 1850, NA RG 75, LS, Minnesota Superintendency; Van Nuys, *Inkpaduta*, 12–13.

43. Pond, *The Dakota*, 69–70; Landes, *Mystic Lake Sioux*, 32, 111; Wozniak, *Contact, Negotiation, and Conflict*, 21–22.

44. Lee, *Spirit Lake Massacre*, 14; Clodfelter, *Dakota War*, 23; Charles Eastman to Herriot, February 3, 1934, FHP.

## CHAPTER 3

1. Hubbard and Holcombe, *Minnesota in Three Centuries*, 3:221; Benjamin Gue, *History of Iowa* (New York: Century History Company, 1903), 1:288; Hughes, *Indian Chiefs of Southern Minnesota*, 129; Herriot, "Indian Massacre," 354; Hughes, "Inkpaduta Massacre," 264; Lee, *Spirit Lake Massacre*, 29.

2. Herriot, "Indian Massacre," 358 360; Harvey Ingham, "Ink-Pa-Du-

Tah's Revenge," *The Midland Monthly* vol IV (July–December, 1895), 271; http://www.ci.pipestone.mn.us/museum/Ink.html; Turning Bear, "Inkpaduta"; *Pipestone County Star*, April 10, 1997; interview with Allard; author's interview with Leonard Wabasha, May 29, 2007.

3. Larson, "New Look," 26; Larson, "Inkpaduta, Renegade Sioux," 10.

4. Diedrich, *Famous Chiefs*, 47; Larson, "Inkpaduta, Renegade Sioux," 18.

5. Larson, "Inkpaduta, Renegade Sioux," 13.

6. Wall, *Iowa*, 23, 25, 34, 38–39, 49.

7. Ibid., 54–55.

8. Hughes, "Inkpaduta Massacre," 264; Flandrau, "Ink-Pa-Du-Ta Massacre of 1857," 386; Bakeman, *Legends, Letters, and Lies*, 11; Roddis, *Indian Wars*, 23; Larson, "New Look," 26.

9. Ingham, "Ink-Pa-Du-Tah's Revenge," 270; Brown, "Spirit Lake Massacre," 1; William Williams, *The History of Early Fort Dodge and Webster County, Iowa* (Fort Dodge, Iowa: KUFD-KFMY, 1950), 13–14; Herriot, "Indian Massacre," 368.

10. Ingham, "Ink-Pa-Du-Tah's Revenge," 270; Hughes, "Inkpaduta Massacre," 265; Brown, "Spirit Lake Massacre," 1.

11. Ingham, "Ink-Pa-Du-Tah's Revenge," 271; Hughes, "Inkpaduta Massacre," 265; Diedrich, *Famous Chiefs*, 48.

12. Williams, *Early Fort Dodge*, 12; Larson, "Inkpaduta, Renegade Sioux," 13; Harvey Ingham, "Sioux Indians Harassed the Early Iowa Settlers," *Annals of Iowa* 34 (1957): 138.

13. Gue, *History of Iowa*, 1:288; Ingham, "Sioux Indians," 138; Taylor, "Inkpaduta and Sons," 153–54.

14. Gue, *History of Iowa*, 1:288; Lee, *Spirit Lake Massacre*, 30; Williams, *Early Fort Dodge*, 12; Hubbard and Holcombe, *Minnesota in Three Centuries*, 3:221.

15. Lee, *Spirit Lake Massacre*, 17; Hubbard and Holcombe, *Minnesota in Three Centuries*, 3:221; Larson, "Inkpaduta, Renegade Sioux," 14; Gue, *History of Iowa*, 1:288; Herriot, "Indian Massacre," 352, 364.

16. Williams, *Early Fort Dodge*, 11; H. M. Pratt, *History of Fort Dodge and Webster County, Iowa* (Chicago: Pioneer Publishing Company, 1913), 151; B. H. Randall, *A Brief Sketch and History of Fort Ridgely* (Fairfax, Minn.: Fairfax Crescent Print, 1896), 4.

17. Williams, *Early Fort Dodge*, 17, 19, 24. Randall, *Brief Sketch of Fort Ridgely*, 4.

18. Williams, *Early Fort Dodge*, 28, 30–31.

19. Blegen, *Minnesota*, 159; Meyer, *History of the Santee Sioux*, 70; Roddis, *Indian Wars*, 1.

20. Journal of the Joint Commission to Treat with the Sioux, 1851, Documents Relating to the Negotiation of Ratified and Unratified Treaties with Various Tribes of Indians (DRNRVT), NA RG 75; Thomas Hughes, "The Treaty of Traverse des Sioux in 1851," *Collections of the Minnesota Historical Society* (1900–1904), 10(1):106; Gary Clayton Anderson, *Little Crow* (St. Paul: Minnesota Historical Society Press, 1986), 53–58.

21. Journal of the Joint Commission to Treat with the Sioux, 1851, DRNRVT, NA RG 75; Blegen, *Minnesota*, 166; Robinson, *History of the Dakota*, 212, 214; Anderson, *Kinsmen of Another Kind*, 181, 201–202.

22. Journal of the Joint Commission to Treat with the Sioux, 1851, DRNRVT, NA RG 75; Robinson, *History of the Dakota*, 213–14; Blegen, *Minnesota*, 166; Anderson, *Kinsmen of Another Kind*, 199.

23. Diedrich, *Famous Chiefs*, 48; Robinson, *History of the Dakota*, 343; Larson, "New Look," 27; Charles Flandrau, "Official Account," April 11, 1857, SED no. 23, 35th Cong., 1st sess., Series 919.

24. Diedrich, *Famous Chiefs*, 48; Wall, *Iowa*, 62.

25. Meyer, *History of the Santee Sioux*, 90, 93; Willis Gorman to Commissioner of Indian Affairs George Manypenny, June 1, July 27, 1853, NA RG 75, LR, Minnesota Superintendency; Gorman to Manypenny, November 15, 28, 1853, NA RG 75, LR, St. Peter Agency; William Prescott to Indian Agent Robert Murphy, September 1, 1853, House Executive Document (HED) no. 1, 33rd Cong., 1st sess., Series 721, 319; Murphy to Mannypenny, May 25, 1855, NA RG 75, LR, Minnesota Superintendency; Wozniak, *Contact, Negotiation, and Conflict*, 10.

26. William Prescott to Gov. Alexander Ramsey, September 23, 1850, NA RG 75, LS, Minnesota Superintendency; Maj. Hannibal Day to Assistant Adjutant General, January 26, 1855, NA RG 393, Letterbook, Fort Ridgely, June 1854–November 1858; Gorman to Manypenny, January 9, 1854, NA RG 75, LS, Minnesota Superintendency; Murphy to Gorman, March 4, August 22, 1854, NA RG 75, LS, Minnesota Superintendency; Meyer, *History of the Santee Sioux*, 92.

27. *St. Peter Courier,* June 14, 1855.

28. Robert Hopkins and Alexander Huggins to Indian Superintendent Thomas Harvey, September 29, 1858, Commissioner of Indian Affairs, *Annual Report*, 1858, 50; Indian Agent Joseph R. Brown to Commissioner of Indian Affairs William Cullen, August 21, 1859, April 15, 1860, NA RG 75, LR, Minnesota Superintendency.

29. Fred Johnson, *A Glimpse of New Ulm* (New Ulm, Minn.: New Ulm Review Print, 1894), 3; Capt. Frederick Steele to Maj. Hannibal Day, August 8, 1855, NA RG 393, LR, Fort Ridgely, 1853–68; Thomas Hughes, *History of Blue Earth County* (Chicago: Middle West Publishing Company, 1909), 32; Office of Indian Affairs, St. Peter Agency, 1855–58, LR, microfilm collection, Minnesota Historical Center, Minnesota State University Library; Evan Jones, *The Minnesota: Forgotten River* (New York: Holt, Rinehart and Winston, 1962), 147–48.

30. Hughes, *History of Blue Earth County*, 55, 63–64; Johnson, *Glimpse of New Ulm*, 5; Jones, *The Minnesota*, 147–48.

31. John Pettijohn to commanding officer, Fort Ridgely, December 20, 1859, NA RG 393, LR, Fort Ridgely.

32. Williams, *Early Fort Dodge*, 76; Larson, "Inkpaduta, Renegade Sioux," 17.

33. Williams, *Early Fort Dodge*, 28.

34. Van Nuys, *Inkpaduta*, 43; Herriot, "Indian Massacre," 365; Diedrich, *Famous Chiefs*, 48.

35. Williams, *Early Fort Dodge*, 81; Ingham, "Sioux Indians," 141.

36. Williams, *Early Fort Dodge*, 81–82; Ingham, "Sioux Indians," 141.

37. Williams, *Early Fort Dodge*, 81–82; Ingham, "Sioux Indians," 139.

38. Martin McLeod Papers, Manuscript Collection, Minnesota Historical Society.

39. Waggoner to Herriot, November 30, 1932, FHP.

40. Miriam Hawthorn Baker, "Inkpaduta's Camp at Smithland," *Annals of Iowa* 39 (Fall 1967): 88, 89; Blank, "Inkpaduatah's Great White Friend," 17–18; Wall, *Iowa*, 63.

41. Diedrich, *Famous Chiefs*, 48; Blank, "Inkpaduatah's Great White Friend," 17.

42. Blank, "Inkpaduatah's Great White Friend," 19.

43. Baker, "Inkpaduta's Camp at Smithland," 89–90.

44. Hughes, *Indian Chiefs of Southern Minnesota*, 130, 134; Larson, "New Look," 26, 27.

45. Diedrich, *Famous Chiefs*, 47.

46. Hughes, *Indian Chiefs of Southern Minnesota*, 135.

47. Wood to the Assistant Adjutant General, August 24, 1853, NA RG 393, LR, Fort Ridgely; Hughes, "Inkpaduta Massacre," 266; Pratt, *History of Fort Dodge*, 153;

48. Lee, *Spirit Lake Massacre*, 20–21.

49. Williams, *Early Fort Dodge*, 87–88.

50. Diedrich, *Famous Chiefs*, 48; Larson, "New Look," 28.

51. Williams, *Early Fort Dodge*, 33; Brown, "Spirit Lake Massacre," 1; Larson, "Inkpaduta, Renegade Sioux," 24; Diedrich, *Famous Chiefs*, 49.

52. Ingham, "Ink-Pa-Du-Tah's Revenge," 271; Brown, "Spirit Lake Massacre," 1; Wall, *Iowa*, 62; Diedrich, *Famous Chiefs*, 49.

53. Diedrich, *Famous Chiefs*, 49; Herriot, "Indian Massacre," 360; Williams, *Early Fort Dodge*, 53; Brown, "Spirit Lake Massacre," 1; Lee, *Spirit Lake Massacre*, 35.

54. Larson, "New Look," 28; Hughes, "Inkpaduta Massacre," 268; Diedrich, *Famous Chiefs*, 49.

55. Hughes, "Inkpaduta Massacre," 268.

56. Herriot, "Indian Massacre," 361, 374; Thomas Teakle, *The Spirit Lake Massacre* (Iowa City: State Historical Society of Iowa, 1918), 35; Hughes, "Inkpaduta Massacre," 267; Willis Gorman to George Manypenny, March 2, 1854, NA RG 75, LS, Minnesota Superintendency.

57. Diedrich, *Famous Chiefs*, 49; Ingham, "Ink-Pa-Du-Tah's Revenge," 16.

58. Hubbard and Holcombe, *Minnesota in Three Centuries*, 3:222–23.

59. Diedrich, *Famous Chiefs*, 46, 49; Brown, "Spirit Lake Massacre," 3; Gue, *History of Iowa*, 1:292.

60. Pond, *The Dakota*, 73.

## CHAPTER 4

1. Diedrich, *Famous Chiefs*, 51; Herriot, "Indian Massacre," 380, 381; Gue, *History of Iowa*, 1:293, 304; Edgar I. Stewart, *Custer's Luck* (Norman: University of Oklahoma Press, 1955), 18.

2. See Paul N. Beck, *The First Sioux War* (Lanham, Md.: University Press of America, 2004).

3. Office of Indian Affairs, St. Peter Agency, *Annual Report*, 1855; Maj. Hannibal Day to Robert Murphy, October 12, 1855, NA RG 393, LS, Fort Ridgely.

4. Morton M. Rosenberg, "The People of Iowa on the Eve of the Civil War," *Annuals of Iowa* 39, no. 2 (Fall 1967): 107, 108–109, 122; Larson, "Inkpaduta, Renegade Sioux," 31; Taylor, "Inkpaduta and Sons," 155; Lee, *Spirit Lake Massacre*, 38, 40.

5. Herriot, "Indian Massacre," 361; Arthur P. Rose, *An Illustrated History of Jackson County, Minnesota* (Jackson, Minn.: Northern History

156 NOTES TO PAGES 56–61

Publishing Company, 1910), 51; Hubbard and Holcombe, *Minnesota in Three Centuries*, 3:220; Lee, *Spirit Lake Massacre*, 14; Doane Robinson Papers; Taylor, "Inkpaduta and Sons," 154.

6. Rose, *Illustrated History*, 50–51; Ingham, "Ink-Pa-Du-Tah's Revenge," 271.

7. Bakeman, *Legends, Letters, and Lies*, 12; Baker, "Inkpaduta's Camp at Smithland," 92.

8. Ingham, "Ink-Pa-Du-Tah's Revenge," 272; R. A. Smith, *A History of Dickerson County, Iowa* (Des Moines: Kenyon Printing and Mfg. Company, 1902), 37; Ambrose Call, "Indians Repelled in Kossuth," *Annals of Iowa* 31 (October 1951): 83; Diedrich, *Famous Chiefs*, 49; Van Nuys, *Inkpaduta*, 33–34, 36–37, 40–41.

9. Kintzing Prichette to Commissioner of Indian Affairs James Denver, October 15, 1857, SED no. 49, 35th Cong., 1st sess., Series 919, 389; Roddis, *Indian Wars*, 22.

10. Taylor, "Inkpaduta and Sons," 155; Larson, "New Look," 29; Prichette to Denver, October 15, 1857, 389; Diedrich, *Famous Chiefs*, 49; Clodfelter, *Dakota War*, 25.

11. Hubbard and Holcombe, *Minnesota in Three Centuries*, 3:253.

12. Larson, "Inkpaduta Renegade Sioux," 32–33.

13. Flandrau, "Official Account," April 11, 1857, SED no. 23, 35th Cong., 1st sess., Series 919, 359; Teakle, *Spirit Lake Massacre*, 69.

14. Roddis, *Indian Wars*, 22; Testimony of Shifting Wind's Wife, SED no. 40, 35th Cong., 1st sess., Series 919; Hubbard and Holcombe, *Minnesota in Three Centuries*, 3:248.

15. Testimony of Shifting Wind's Wife, SED no. 40, 35th Cong., 1st sess., Series 919; Hubbard and Holcombe, *Minnesota in Three Centuries*, 3:248; Baker, "Inkpaduta's Camp at Smithland," 83.

16. David L. Bristow, "Inkpaduta's Revenge: The True Story of the Spirit Lake Massacre," *The Iowan* (January–February 1999), http://members.aol.com/dlbristow/inkpadut.htm; Smith, *History of Dickerson County, Iowa*, 49.

17. Rose, *Illustrated History*, 51; Taylor, "Inkpaduta and Sons," 155–56.

18. Clark, "Spirit Lake Massacre," 1; Hughes, "Inkpaduta Massacre," 270; Curtis Harnack, "Prelude to Massacre," *Iowan* 4 (February–March, 1956): 36; Diedrich, *Famous Chiefs*, 50.

19. Wall, *Iowa*, 62; Harnack, "Prelude to Massacre," 36–37.

20. Van Nuys, *Inkpaduta*, 57–58, 60; Baker, "Inkpaduta's Camp at Smithland," 92.

21. Baker, "Inkpaduta's Camp at Smithland," 82, 83, 85, 87, 90–91; Wallace Adams to Frank Herriot, August 26, 1932, FHP.

22. Hubbard and Holcombe, *Minnesota in Three* Centuries, 3:223; Rose, *Illustrated History*, 52; Baker, "Inkpaduta's Camp at Smithland," 90, 91.

23. Baker, "Inkpaduta's Camp at Smithland," 90.

24. Wallace Adams to Frank Herriot, August 1, 1933, FHP; Baker, "Inkpaduta's Camp at Smithland," 90.

25. Adams to Herriot, August 26, 1932, FHP; Baker, "Inkpaduta's Camp at Smithland," 83.

26. Taylor, "Inkpaduta and Sons," 155–56; Diedrich, *Famous Chiefs*, 49–50.

27. Waggoner to Frank Herriot, November 30, 1932, FHP; Brown, "Spirit Lake Massacre," 4; Baker, "Inkpaduta's Camp at Smithland," 1–3.

28. Taylor, "Inkpaduta and Sons," 156; Baker, "Inkpaduta's Camp at Smithland," 93–94.

29. Taylor, "Inkpaduta and Sons," 157; Baker, "Inkpaduta's Camp at Smithland," 94–95; Diedrich, *Famous Chiefs*, 50–51.

30. Robinson, *History of the Dakota*, 233.

31. Folwell, *History of Minnesota*, 2:401; Diedrich, *Famous Chiefs*, 50; Baker, "Inkpaduta's Camp at Smithland," 96; interview with Allard; interview with Wabasha; interview with Little Ghost; interview with Seaboy.

32. Baker, "Inkpaduta's Camp at Smithland," 97–99.

33. Taylor, "Inkpaduta and Sons," 158.

34. Rose, *Illustrated History*, 52; Clark, "Spirit Lake Massacre," 6; Robinson, *History of the Dakota*, 234; Wall, *Iowa*, 63; Harnack, "Prelude to Massacre," 38.

35. *Pipestone County Star*, April 10, 1997; Hughes, "Inkpaduta Massacre," 269; Rose, *Illustrated History*, 53–54.

36. Brown, "Spirit Lake Massacre," 4; Gue, *History of Iowa*, 1:294; Lee, *Spirit Lake Massacre*, 92; Bakeman, *Legends, Letters, and Lies*, 29.

37. Larson, "Inkpaduta, Renegade Sioux," 36.

38. Taylor, "Inkpaduta and Sons," 153; Herriot, "Indian Massacre," 342; Lee, *Spirit Lake Massacre*, 44; Wall, *Iowa*, 61.

39. Lee, *Spirit Lake Massacre*, 7, 9; William Peterson, "The Spirit Lake Massacre," *Palimpsest* 38 (June 1957): 210.

40. Lee, *Spirit lake Massacre*, 53; Bakeman, *Legends, Letters, and Lies*, 25.

41. Bakeman, *Legends, Letters, and Lies*, 25; Clark, "Spirit Lake Mas-

sacre," 2; Frank Herriot, "Dr. Isaac H. Harriott," *Annals of Iowa* 18 (1932): 260, 281, 283–87; Lee, *Spirit lake Massacre*, 53–54.

42. Lee, *Spirit Lake Massacre*, 55; Laut, "Pioneer Women of the West," 686–87.

43. Brown, "Spirit Lake Massacre," 4; Larson, "Inkpaduta, Renegade Sioux," 37; Lee, *Spirit Lake Massacre*, 94.

44. Abigail Gardner Sharp, *History of the Spirit Lake Massacre* (Des Moines: Wallace-Homestead Book Company, 1971), 67–68; Lee, *Spirit Lake Massacre*, 96, 97.

45. Hughes, "Inkpaduta Massacre," 271; Clark, "Spirit Lake Massacre," 7; Brown, "Spirit Lake Massacre," 4; Petersen, "Spirit Lake Massacre," 226; Lee, *Spirit Lake Massacre*, 15–16.

46. Sharp, *Spirit Lake Massacre*, 69; Petersen, "Spirit Lake Massacre," 226; Hughes, "Inkpaduta Massacre," 271–72; Herriot, "Dr. IsaacH. Harriott," 257.

47. Sharp, *Spirit Lake Massacre*, 70–71; Brown, "Spirit Lake Massacre," 4; Clark, "Spirit Lake Massacre," 7; Lee, *Spirit Lake Massacre*, 100.

48. Sharp, *Spirit Lake Massacre*, 72–73; Lee, *Spirit Lake Massacre*, 100; Hughes, "Inkpaduta Massacre," 272; Clark, "Spirit Lake Massacre," 7; Brown, "Spirit Lake Massacre," 4.

49. Lee, *Spirit Lake Massacre*, 104; Hughes, "Inkpaduta Massacre," 272; Hubbard and Holcombe, *Minnesota in Three Centuries*, 3:219; Roddis, *Indian Wars*, 24.

50. Brown, "Spirit Lake Massacre," 5.

51. Sharp, *Spirit Lake Massacre*, 80; Bakeman, *Legends, Letters, and Lies*, 25; Lee, *Spirit Lake Massacre*, 108–109; Brown, "Spirit Lake Massacre," 5; Sharp, *Spirit Lake Massacre*, 60.

52. Brown, "Spirit Lake Massacre," 5; Lee, *Spirit Lake Massacre*, 110.

53. Brown, "Spirit Lake Massacre," 5–6; Lee, *Spirit Lake Massacre*, 110.

54. Roddis, *Indian Wars*, 24.

55. Ibid., 25–26; Lee, *Spirit Lake Massacre*, 113, 115.

56. Brown, "Spirit Lake Massacre," 6–7; Lee, *Spirit Lake Massacre*, 115–17.

# CHAPTER 5

1. Flandrau, "Ink-Pa-Du-Ta Massacre of 1857," 3:407; Lee, *Spirit Lake Massacre*, 67.

2. Clodfelter, *Dakota War*, 25; Van Nuys, *Inkpaduta*, i.

3. Orlando C. Howe, "The Discovery of the Spirit Lake Massacre," *Annals of Iowa* 11 (July 1914): 420; Lee, *Spirit Lake Massacre*, 122; Hughes, "Inkpaduta Massacre," 272–73; Laut, "Pioneer Women of the West," 690.

4. Howe, "Discovery of the Spirit Lake Massacre," 408–11; Clark, "Spirit Lake Massacre," 14–15.

5. Howe, "Discovery of the Spirit Lake Massacre," 412, 414, 416.

6. Ibid., 416–17, 419–20, 421.

7. Ibid., 423–24.

8. Hubbard and Holcombe, *Minnesota in Three Centuries*, 3:225; Lee, *Spirit Lake Massacre*, 56, 132; Roddis, *Indian Wars*, 27–28.

9. Larson, "New Look," 30; Hubbard and Holcombe, *Minnesota in Three Centuries*, 3:226; Lee, *Spirit Lake Massacre*, 136–37.

10. Flandrau, "Ink-Pa-Du-Ta Massacre of 1857," 3:388; Folwell, *History of Minnesota*, 2:223; Teakle, *Spirit Lake Massacre*, 128, 130; Rose, *Illustrated History*, 75; Daniel Buck, *Indian Outbreaks* (Minneapolis: Ross and Haines, 1965), 35; Charles Flandrau to Francis Huebschmann, March 19, 1857, NA RG 75, LR, St. Peter Agency.

11. Roddis, *Indian Wars*, 29; Hubbard and Holcombe, *Minnesota in Three Centuries*, 3:228.

12. Lee, *Spirit Lake Massacre*, 119; Roddis, *Indian Wars*, 27, 29; Hubbard and Holcombe, *Minnesota in Three Centuries*, 3:219, 226.

13. Hughes, "Inkpaduta Massacre," 275; Rose, *Illustrated History*, 60.

14. Lee, *Spirit Lake Massacre*, 20.

15. Roddis, *Indian Wars*, 29–30; Lee, *Spirit Lake Massacre*, 138–40; Hubbard and Holcombe, *Minnesota in Three Centuries*, 3:229.

16. Hubbard and Holcombe, *Minnesota in Three Centuries*, 3:229, 231–32.

17. Hughes, "Inkpaduta Massacre," 275; Rose, *Illustrated History*, 62–63; Hubbard and Holcombe, *Minnesota in Three Centuries*, 3:230; Lee, *Spirit Lake Massacre*, 143–44.

18. Rose, *Illustrated History*, 65; Hubbard and Holcombe, *Minnesota in Three Centuries*, 3:230–31; Lee, *Spirit Lake Massacre*, 144.

19. Lee, *Spirit Lake Massacre*, 142; Hubbard and Holcombe, *Minnesota in Three Centuries*, 3:231–32; *Henderson Democrat*, May 7, 1857.

20. Larson, "Inkpaduta, Renegade Sioux," 46.

21. Hughes, "Inkpaduta Massacre," 276–77; Hubbard and Holcombe, *Minnesota in Three Centuries*, 3:234.

22. Clark, "Spirit Lake Massacre," 8, 16–19.

23. Ibid., 20–21.

24. Herriot, "Dr. Isaac H. Harriott," 256; Lee, *Spirit Lake Massacre,* 32.

25. Clark, "Spirit Lake Massacre," 22, 26; Hubbard and Holcombe, *Minnesota in Three Centuries,* 3:224–25.

26. Anonymous, *Fort Ridgely, Minnesota* (Washington, D.C.: War Department, Office of Secretary of War, Adj. Gen. Fletcher Williams, 1880), Bee's Report, April 9, 1857; Rose, *Illustrated History,* 79.

27. Hughes, "Inkpaduta Massacre," 273; Jones, *The Minnesota,* 178; Teakle, *Spirit Lake Massacre,* 129–30.

28. Anonymous, *Fort Ridgely, Minnesota,* Bee's Report, April 9, 1857.

29. Hughes, "Inkpaduta Massacre," 276; Anonymous, *Fort Ridgely, Minnesota,* Bee's Report, April 9, 1857; Roddis, *Indian Wars,* 33–35; Diedrich, *Famous Chiefs,* 51.

30. Anonymous, *Fort Ridgely, Minnesota,* Bee's Report, April 9, 1857; Hughes, "Inkpaduta Massacre," 277; Teakle, *Spirit Lake Massacre,* 158.

31. *St. Paul Daily Pioneer and Democrat,* March 25 and 26, 1857; *Des Moines Citizen,* April 2, 1857; *Henderson Democrat,* March 26, April 16, May 7, 1857; *St. Paul Advertiser,* April 18, 1857; *St. Peter Courier,* May 20, 1857.

32. *St. Paul Daily Times,* April 15 and 16, 1857; Hughes, "Inkpaduta Massacre," 280; *St. Anthony Express,* April 18, 1857; *St. Peter Courier,* May 12, 1857; *Oskaloosa Herald,* May 8, 1857.

33. Flandrau to Huebschmann, April 16, 1857, NA RG 75, LR, St. Peter Agency; Frank Herriot, "Aftermath of the Spirit Lake Massacre," *Annals of Iowa* 18 (1932): 493–94, 495–96.

34. Charles Flandrau to Superintendent of Indian Affairs Francis Huebschmann, April 16, 1857, SED no. 24, 35th Cong., 1st sess., Series 919, 360; Folwell, *History of Minnesota,* 2:224; TheodoreG. Carver and Family Papers, Manuscript Collection, Minnesota Historical Society; *Winona Republican,* April 20, 1857.

35. J. A. Nelson to [unclear], April 19, 1857, J. A. Nelson Letters, Manuscript Collection, Minnesota Historical Society; Hubbard and Holcombe, *Minnesota in Three Centuries,* 3:245, 247; *Minnesota Pioneer and Democrat,* April 23, 1857; TheodoreE. Potter, "Recollections of Minnesota Experiences," *Minnesota History Bulletin* 2 (1917–18): 433; Thomas Scantlebury Diaries, April 17, 1857, Manuscript Collection, Minnesota Historical Society; Jones, *The Minnesota,* 176; *St. Paul Daily Times,* April 17, 1857.

36. Edward Washburn to father, April 27, 1857, Edward and Wil-

liam Washburn Letters, Manuscript Collection, Minnesota Historical Society.

37. *Chicago Democratic Press*, April 23, 1857; *New York Daily Tribune*, May 25, 1857; Francis Huebschmann to James Denver, May 8, 1857, Commissioner of Indian Affairs, *Annual Report*, 1857.

38. *Henderson Democrat*, April 16, 1857; William B. Dodd Papers, Manuscript Collection, Minnesota Historical Society.

39. *St. Paul Advertiser*, April 18, 1857; Huebschmann to Denver, April 14, 1857, NA RG 75, LR, St. Peter Agency; Hubbard and Holcombe, *Minnesota in Three Centuries*, 3:245–46.

40. Hubbard and Holcombe, *Minnesota in Three Centuries*, 3:245–46; Van Nuys, *Inkpaduta*, 90.

41. Hughes, "Inkpaduta Massacre," 278–79; Hubbard and Holcombe, *Minnesota in Three Centuries*, 3:243–44; Roddis, *Indian Wars*, 47.

42. *Henderson Democrat*, April 16, 1857; *St. Paul Daily Times*, April 17, 1857; Hughes, "Inkpaduta Massacre," 278–79; Hubbard and Holcombe, *Minnesota in Three Centuries*, 3:244.

43. Hughes, "Inkpaduta Massacre," 279–80; Hubbard and Holcombe, *Minnesota in Three Centuries* 3:244–45; Roddis, *Indian Wars*, 47.

44. Huebschmann to Denver, May 8, 1857, NA RG 75, LR, St. Peter Agency; Edward Washburn to father, April 27, 1857, Edward and William Washburn Letters; Hughes, *Indian Chiefs of Southern Minnesota*, 107, Larson, "New Look," 33; Hubbard and Holcombe, *Minnesota in Three Centuries*, 3:245.

45. Letter, Thomas Cowan to Colonel Alexander, April 18, 1857, NA RG 393, LR, Fort Ridgely; Larson, "New Look," 33.

46. Larson, "Inkpaduta, Renegade Sioux," 53; Harold Peterson, "Wahkonsa," *Palimpsest* 23 (April 1942): 133–34.

47. Herriot, "Aftermath of Spirit Lake," 464; Larson, "New Look," 31.

48. *Henderson Democrat*, May 7, July 16, 1857; *St. Peter Courier*, May 6, 1857.

49. *St. Peter Courier*, May 20, 1857.

50. *St. Peter (Minnesota) Free Press*, July 29, 1857; Anonymous, *Fort Ridgely, Minnesota*, Alexander to Assistant Adjutant General, April 12, 1857.

51. *Brownsville Southern Minnesota Herald*, May 9, 1857; A. Robertson to Charles Flandrau, April 10, 1857, Charles Flandrau Papers, Manuscript Collection, Minnesota Historical Society; Hubbard and Holcombe, *Minnesota in Three Centuries*, 3:249.

52. Sharp, *Spirit Lake Massacre*, 156; 161; *Pipestone County Star*, April 10, 1997; Robinson, *History of the Dakota*, 237.

53. Sharp, *Spirit Lake Massacre*, 83–84, 158; Margaret Marble to James Denver, July 23, 1857, "Petition for loss of Property," NA RG 75, LR, St. Peter Agency; Clark, "Spirit Lake Massacre," 24–25; Lee, *Spirit Lake Massacre*, 23.

54. Sharp, *Spirit Lake Massacre*, 160; Roddis, *Indian Wars*, 37; Hubbard and Holcombe, *Minnesota in Three Centuries*, 3:235; Laut, "Pioneer Women of the West," 692, 694; Brown, "Spirit Lake Massacre," 11; Riggs, *Tah-Koo Wah-Kan*, 49.

55. Lee, *Spirit Lake Massacre*, 22; Diedrich, *Famous Chiefs*, 51.

56. Flandrau to Commissioner of Indian Affairs, September 24, 1857, *Annual Report*, 1857, 58; Riggs, *Tah-Koo Wah-Kan*, 265; Roddis, *Indian Wars*, 38; Robinson, *History of the Dakotas*, 237–38.

57. Riggs, *Tah-Koo Wah-Kan*, 266; Flandrau, "Ink-Pa-Du-Ta Massacre of 1857," 3:394; Lee, *Spirit Lake Massacre*, 26.

58. Hubbard and Holcombe, *Minnesota in Three Centuries*, 3:236; Sharp, *Spirit Lake Massacre*, 226–31; Laut, "Pioneer Women of the West," 696.

59. "Narrative of Paul Mazakootemane," *Collections of the Minnesota Historical Society* (1880), 3:82–83; H.H. Sibley, "Sketch of John Other Day," *Collections of the Minnesota Historical Society* (1880), 3:99–100; Hughes, *Indian Chiefs of Southern Minnesota*, 82.

60. *Faribault Herald*, July 2, 1857; Flandrau, "Ink-Pa-Du-Ta Massacre of 1857," 3:393; Lee, *Spirit Lake Massacre*, 33–34; Larson, "New Look," 31.

61. Lee, *Spirit Lake Massacre*, 35, 42; *Fairbault Herald*, July 2, 1857.

62. Meyer, *History of the Santee Sioux*, 101; Anderson, *Kinsmen of Another Kind*, 221, 226; G. Hubert Papers, Manuscript Collection, Minnesota Historical Society; Van Nuys, *Inkpaduta*, 156.

## CHAPTER 6

1. Robinson, *History of the Dakota*, 346.

2. Ibid., 344; Clodfelter, *Dakota War*, 23.

3. FHP; Lee, *Spirit Lake Massacre*, 70.

4. Robinson, *History of the Dakota*, 344; Kintzing Prichette to James Denver, August 5, 1857, 35th Cong., 1st sess., SED 36, Serial 919, 86; *Henderson Democrat*, June 25, 1857.

5. Flandrau, "Ink-Pa-Du-Ta Massacre of 1857," 3:402–403; Charles Flandrau to Superintendent William Cullen, September 24, 1857, SED no. 18, 35th Cong., 1st sess., Series 919, 346; Prichette to Denver, October 15, 1857, 391; Jones, *The Minnesota*, 179; Roddis, *Indian Wars*, 42.

6. Flandrau, "Ink-Pa-Du-Ta Massacre of 1857," 3:405; Robinson, *History of the Dakota*, 241–42.

7. Flandrau, "Ink-Pa-Du-Ta Massacre of 1857," 3:406; Prichette to Denver, October 15, 1857, 392; Anderson, *Kinsmen of Another Kind*, 219.

8. Kinzting Prichette to James Denver, October 15, 1857, Commissioner of Indian Affairs, *Annual Report* (Washington, D.C.: William A. Harris Printer, 1857); Assistant Adjutant General L. Thomas to Commanding General Winfield Scott, August 3, 1857, SED no. 11, 35th Cong., 1st sess., Series 920; *St. Peter Minnesota Free Press*, July 22, 1857; Stephen Riggs to Charles Flandrau, July 1, 1857, Charles Flandrau Papers.

9. Roddis, *Indian Wars*, 44; Folwell, *History of Minnesota*, 2:410; William Cullen to James Denver, July 15, 1857, 35th Cong., 1st sess., SED no. 29, Serial 919, 74–75; William Cullen to James Denver, July 26, 1857, SED no. 33, 35th Cong., 1st sess., Series 919, 81.

10. Cullen to Denver, July 26, 1857, 79, 81; Hubbard and Holcombe, *Minnesota in Three Centuries*, 3:263; Roddis, *Indian Wars*, 45; Anderson, *Kinsmen of Another Kind*, 219.

11. Kintzing Prichette to James Denver, August 7, 1857, 35th Cong., 1st sess., SED no. 37, Series 919, 88; Roddis, *Indian Wars*, 45–46; Report of A.J. Campbell, SED no. 38, 35th Cong., 1st sess., Series 919, 374–76; Sibley, "Sketch of John Other Day," 100.

12. Prichette to Denver, October 15, 1857, 387–88.

13. Flandrau, "Ink-Pa-Du-Ta Massacre of 1857," 3:396–97; *St. Paul Pioneer Press*, August 1896; *St. Paul Pioneer and Democrat*, July 19, 1857.

14. James Denver to Kintzing Prichette, July 22, 1857; SED no. 32, 35th Cong., 1st sess., Series 919, 77; Hubbard and Holcombe, *Minnesota in Three Centuries*, 3:251–52.

15. Lt. Col. John Abercrombie to Capt. H. C. Pratt, August 30, September 16, 1857, NA RG 393, Letterbook, Fort Ridgely, June 1854–November 1858; Capt. H. C. Pratt to Lt. Col. John Abercrombie, September 15, 1857, NA RG 393, LR, Fort Ridgely.

16. Capt. Alfred Sully to Lieutenant Ruggles, October 23, 1857, NA RG 393, LR, Fort Ridgely.

17. Diedrich, *Famous Chiefs*, 52; *Fairbault Herald*, July 2, 1857; Lee, *Spirit Lake Massacre*, 36; Prichette to Denver, August 7, 1857, 375; Larson, "Inkpaduta, Renegade Sioux," 70.

18.  *Sioux City Eagle*, June 12, 1858; Larson, "Inkpaduta, Renegade Sioux," 70–71.

19.  Diedrich, *Famous Chiefs*, 52; Samuel J. Albright, "The First Organized Government of Dakota," *Collections of the Minnesota Historical Society* (1898), 8:140.

20.  Herriot, "Aftermath of Spirit Lake," 506; Larson, "New Look," 33; Larson, "Inkpaduta, Renegade Sioux," 70.

21.  Hoover, *Yankton Sioux*, 30; Herbert S. Schell, *History of South Dakota* (Lincoln: University of Nebraska Press, 1975), 71–72; Robinson, *History of the Dakota*, 246–49.

22.  *St. Peter (Minnesota) Free Press*, August 10, 11, and 17, 1859.

23.  Diedrich, *Famous Chiefs*, 52; Gov. H. H. Sibley to Maj. W. W. Morris, October 29, 1859, NA RG 393, LR, Fort Ridgely; Sibley to Morris, December 29, 1859, NA RG 393, LR, Fort Ridgely.

24.  Diedrich, *Famous Chiefs*, 52.

25.  *St. Cloud Democrat*, June 13, 1861.

26.  Indian Agent Thomas Galbraith to Indian Superintendent Clark Thompson, October 1, 1861, SED no. 30, 37th Cong., 2nd sess., Series 1117, 703.

27.  *Mankato Semi-Weekly Record*, August 27, September 10, 1861.

28.  Diedrich, *Famous Chiefs*, 52; Hubbard and Holcombe, *Minnesota in Three Centuries*, 3:292.

29.  Hubbard and Holcombe, *Minnesota in Three Centuries*, 3:292; Larson, "New Look," 33.

30.  Timothy J. Sheehan, Diary, July 27, 1862, Manuscript Collection, Minnesota Historical Society; Robinson, *History of the Dakota*, 266.

31.  Board of Commissioners, comp., *Minnesota in the Civil War and Indian Wars* (St. Paul: Pioneer Press Company, 1899), 2:176; Thomas Patrick Gere Journal, 1862–1865, Manuscript Collection, Minnesota Historical Society, July 28, 1862; Robinson, *History of the Dakota*, 266; Sheehan, Diary, July 27, 1862; Hubbard and Holcombe, *Minnesota in Three Centuries*, 3:292.

32.  Sheehan, Diary, August 4 and 6–9, 1862; Thomas Galbraith to Superintendent Clark Thompson, January 27, 1863, HED no. 1, 38th Cong., 1st sess., Series 1182, 389; Anderson, *Little Crow*, 123, 127–28; Duane Schultz, *Over the Earth I Come: The Great Sioux Uprising of 1862* (New York: St. Martin's Press, 1992), 27–28.

33.  Meyer, *History of the Santee Sioux*, 115; Gary Clayton Anderson and Alan R. Woolworth, eds., *Through Dakota Eyes: Narrative Accounts of the Minnesota Indian War of 1862* (St. Paul: Minnesota Historical Society,

1986), 19–20; Schultz, *Over the Earth I Come*, 6; Kenneth Carley, *The Sioux Uprising of 1862* (St. Paul: Minnesota Historical Society, 1961), 5.

34. Anderson and Woolworth, *Through Dakota Eyes*, 19–20; Return I. Holcombe, "Chief Big Eagle's Story of the Sioux Outbreak of 1862," *Collections of the Minnesota Historical Society* (1894), 6:384–85; Carley, *Sioux Uprising of 1862*, 5.

35. Carley, *Sioux Uprising of 1862*, 5; Isaac Heard, *History of the Sioux War and Massacres of 1862 and 1863* (New York: Harper and Brothers Publishers, 1865), 46; Asa Daniels, "Reminiscences of Little Crow," *Collections of the Minnesota Historical Society* (1908), 12:520; Roddis, *Indian Wars*, 46, 55; Riggs, *Tah-Koo Wah-Kan*, 278; Robinson, *History of the Dakota*, 268; Hubbard and Holcombe, *Minnesota in Three Centuries*, 3:254; Anderson, *Kinsmen of Another Kind*, 231; Folwell, *History of Minnesota*, 2:225, 408.

36. Anderson, *Little Crow*, 130–39; Schultz, *Over the Earth I Come*, 48–58; Heard, *History of the Sioux War*, 73; Board of Commissioners, *Minnesota in the Civil War*, 2:112–14, 166–81.

37. Robinson, *History of the Dakota*, 244; Doane Robison Papers; Waggoner to Herriot, December 30, 1932, FHP; Larson, "New Look," 33.

38. Waggoner to Herriot, December 30, 1932, FHP; Larson, "New Look," 34.

39. Heard, *History of the Sioux War*, 99; Doane Robinson Papers; Roddis, *Indian Wars*, 74; Buck, *Indian Outbreaks*, 99.

40. *St. Paul Daily Press*, February 5, 1863.

41. Clodfelter, *Dakota War*, 25; James Welch and Paul Stekler, *Killing Custer: The Battle of the Little Big Horn and the Fate of the Plains Indians* (New York: W. W. Norton, 1994), 111–12; Roddis, *Indian Wars*, 9–10.

42. Meyer, *History of the Santee Sioux*, 121–23; Carley, *Sioux Uprising of 1862*, 61–65; Schultz, *Over the Earth I Come*, 231–33, 239.

43. Doane Robinson Papers; Robert M. Utley, *Frontiersmen in Blue: The United States Army and the Indian, 1848–1865* (Lincoln: University of Nebraska Press, 1981), 268–69.

44. Anderson, *Kinsmen of Another Kind,* 278; Howard, *Canadian Sioux*, 25; Welch and Stekler, *Killing Custer*, 112; Gue, *History of Iowa*, 1:327; Doane Robinson Papers; Robinson, *History of the Dakota*, 344.

45. George W. Kinsbury, *History of Dakota Territory* (Chicago: S. J. Clarke Publishing Company, 1915), 1:112–13; *Yankton Weekly Dakotan*, November 11, 1862.

46. Robinson, *History of the Dakota*, 314; Diedrich, *Famous Chiefs*, 52–53.

47. Clodfelter, *Dakota War*, 120–23; Jerry Keenan, *The Great Sioux Uprising: Rebellion on the Plains, August–September 1862* (Cambridge, Mass.: Da Capo Press, 2003), 83–84.

48. American Battlefield Protection Program, http://www.nps.gov/history/hps/abpp/battles/nd004.htm; American Civil War.com, State Battle Maps, North Dakota, "September 3–5, 1863 Whitestone Hill," http://www.americancivilwar.com/statepic/nd/nd004.html; Clodfelter, *Dakota War*, 132–33; Van Nuys, *Inkpaduta*, 262, 277, 286.

49. Turning Bear, "Inkpaduta Santee, 1815–1882," *Fort Peck Assiniboine and Sioux History* (1900), http://www.montana.edu/wwwfpcc/tribes/santee.html; Larson, "New Look," 34; Van Nuys, *Inkpaduta*, 264–65, 444.

50. Folwell, *History of Minnesota*, 1:429; Larson, "New Look," 34.

51. Clodfelter, *Dakota War*, 128; Robinson, *History of the Dakota*, 318; Diedrich, *Famous Chiefs*, 53.

52. Robinson, *History of the Dakota*, 318; Clodfelter, *Dakota War*, 94–95; Doane Robinson Papers; Hughes, *Indian Chiefs of Southern Minnesota*, 124–25.

53. Robinson, *History of the Dakota*, 319, 321–22.

54. Ibid., 322; Larson, "New Look," 34; Doane Robinson Papers; Clodfelter, *Dakota War*, 62, 89, 101.

55. U.S. War Department, *The War of the Rebellion: A Compilation of the Official Records of the Union and Confederate Armies* (Hereafter cited as *O.R.*), ser. 1, vol. 22, pt. 1 (Washington, D.C., 1880), Report of Gen. Henry Sibley, August 7, 1863, 355–56; Clodfelter, *Dakota War*, 111; Robinson, *History of the Dakota*, 323–24.

56. *Yankton Weekly Dakotan*, July 28, 1863; *Yankton Press and Dakotan*, November 2, 1998; Mildred Throne, ed., "Iowa Troops in Dakota Territory, 1861–1864," *Iowa Journal of History* 57 (April 1959): 162.

57. Throne, "Iowa Troops in Dakota Territory," 163; *Yankton Press and Dakotan*, November 2, 1998; Robinson, *History of the Dakota*, 345.

58. *O.R.*, ser. 1, vol. 22, pt. 1, Report of Maj. Albert House, September 3, 1863, 564; Doane Robinson Papers; Diedrich, *Famous Chiefs*, 53; Clodfelter, *Dakota War*, 129–33.

59. Robinson, *History of the Dakota*, 327; Van Nuys, *Inkpaduta*, 301; Clodfelter, *Dakota War*, 4–5.

60. *O.R.*, ser. 1, vol. 22, pt. 1, Report of Gen. Alfred Sully, September 11, 1863, 555–60; Waggoner to Herriot, August 25, 1933, FHP; interview with Allard; interview with Little Ghost; Clair Jacobson, "The Battle of Whitestone Hill," *North Dakota History* 44 (Spring 1977): 12;

Diedrich, *Famous Chiefs*, 53; Robinson, *History of the Dakota*, 328, 345; Clodfelter, *Dakota War*, 143–44.

61. Doane Robinson Papers; Clodfelter, *Dakota War*, 147; Larson, "Inkpaduta, Renegade Sioux," 80.

62. Interview with Little Ghost; interview with Allard.

## CHAPTER 7

1. Robinson, *History of the Dakota*, 327, 345; Diedrich, *Famous Chiefs*, 53.

2. Clodfelter, *Dakota War*, 160–61; Robert M. Utley, *The Lance and the Shield: The Life and Times of Sitting Bull* (New York: Henry Holt Company, 1993), 54.

3. Clodfelter, *Dakota War*, 161; Doane Robinson Papers; Diedrich, *Famous Chiefs*, 53; Larson, "Inkpaduta, Renegade Sioux," 83; interview with Allard.

4. Utley, *Lance and Shield*, 55; Clodfelter, *Dakota War*, 164; Van Nuys, *Inkpaduta*, 323; Robinson, *History of the Dakota*, 335; Diedrich, *Famous Chiefs*, 53.

5. *O.R.* ser. 1, vol. 41, pt. 2, Report of Gen. Alfred Sully, July 31, 1864; Clodfelter, *Dakota War*, 168–70.

6. Clodfelter, *Dakota War*, 170–71; Utley, *Lance and Shield*, 56.

7. Clodfelter, *Dakota War*, 176–77.

8. FHP; Diedrich, *Famous Chiefs*, 54.

9. Board of Commissioners, *Minnesota in the Civil and Indian Wars*, 2:548–49; GeorgeW. Doud Diary, August 31, 1864, Manuscript Collection, Minnesota Historical Society; Diedrich, *Famous Chiefs*, 54.

10. Howard, *Canadian Sioux*, 26, 28; Jacobson, "Yantonai and Hunkpatina Sioux," 22; Roy Meyer, "The Canadian Sioux: Refugees from Minnesota," *Minnesota History* 41 (Spring 1968): 13.

11. Robinson, *History of the Dakota*, 390; Diedrich, *Famous Chiefs*, 54–55.

12. Robinson, *History of the Dakota*, 390; Waggoner to Herriot, FHP; Diedrich, *Famous Chiefs*, 54.

13. Clodfelter, *Dakota War*, 26; Robinson, *History of the Dakota*, 346, 360; Doane Robinson Papers.

14. Taylor, *Twenty Years*, 47.

15. Gibbon, *The Sioux*, 5; Winifred W. Barton, *JohnP. Williamson: A Brother to the Sioux* (Clements, Minn.: Sunnycrest Publishing, 1980), 74–

75, 78, 80, 84, 87–89; Letter, J. P. Williamson to his mother, March 2, 1864, *Minnesota Archaeologist* 20, no. 1 (January 1956): 5–6.

16. Larson, "Inkpaduta, Renegade Sioux," 84; Richard G. Hardorff, ed., *Lakota Recollections of the Custer Fight* (Spokane, Wash.: Arthur H. Clark Company, 1991), 78n17; John S. Gray, *Centennial Campaign: The Sioux War of 1876* (Fort Collins, Colo.: Old Army Press, 1976), 328; Thomas Marquis to Frank Herriot, January 13, 1934, FHP; Diedrich, *Famous Chiefs*, 55.

17. Waggoner to Herriot, January 12, 1934, FHP; interview with He Dog, in *Custer in '76: Walter Camp's Notes on the Custer Fight*, ed. Kenneth Hammer (Provo, Utah: Brigham Young University, 1976), 206; Gray, *Centennial Campaign*, 328; Utley, *Lance and Shield*, 134; David Humphreys Miller, *Custer's Fall: The Native American Side of the Story* (New York: Meridan Press, 1992), 224; Hardorff, *Lakota Recollections*, 38; Diedrich, *Famous Chiefs*, 55.

18. Jerome A. Greene, ed., *Lakota and Cheyenne: Indian Views of the Great Sioux War, 1876–1877* (Norman: University of Oklahoma Press, 1994), 33; "Crazy Horse's Story of the Custer Fight," *South Dakota Historical Collections* (1912), 6:226; Robinson, *History of the Dakota*, 429.

19. Brown, "Spirit Lake Massacre," 11; interview with Little Ghost; Hubbard and Holcombe, *Minnesota in Three Centuries*, 3:267; interview with Seaboy.

20. Diedrich, *Famous Chiefs*, 60n71; Waggoner to Herriot, February 15, 1933, FHP; Van Nuys, *Inkpaduta*, 397; Lawrence Fox to Frank Herriot, February 16, 1932, FHP; Robinson, *History of the Dakota*, 430–31.

21. Van Nuys, *Inkpaduta*, 398–99.

22. Greene, *Lakota and Cheyenne*, 35; Hardorff, *Lakota Recollections*, 121; Eastman to Herriot, February, 3, 1934, FHP; Stewart, *Custer's Luck*, 17; Miller, *Custer's Fall*, 178, 210; Diedrich, *Famous Chiefs*, 56.

23. John Coward, *The Newspaper Indian: Native American Identity in the Press, 1820–90* (Urbana: University of Illinois Press, 1999), 163, 165.

24. Gray, *Centennial Campaign*, 242, 249.

25. G. M. Matheson, Canadian Department of Indian Affairs, to Frank Herriot, October 1933, FHP; Waggoner to Herriot, December 23, 1932, FHP; interview with Little Ghost; Diedrich, *Famous Chiefs*, 56, 60n74; Larson, "New Look," 35; interview with Seaboy.

26. Waggoner to Herriot, March 3, 1932, FHP; Larson, "New Look," 35; Diedrich, *Famous Chiefs*, 56.

27. Waggoner to Herriot, March 3, 1932, April 13, September 8,

1934, FHP; Diedrich, *Famous Chiefs*, 56; Laut, "Pioneer Women of the West," 698; Larson, "Inkpaduta, Renegade Sioux," 90.

28. Philip F. Wells, "Ninety-six Years among the Indians of the Northwest — Adventures and Reminiscences of an Indian Scout and Interpreter in the Dakotas," *North Dakota Historical Quarterly* 15, no. 2 (April 1948): 130–32; interview with Seaboy; interview with Allard.

29. Waggoner to Herriot, August 13, 1933, FHP.

30. Interview with Seaboy.

31. Ibid.; interview with Allard.

# Bibliography

## PRIMARY SOURCES

### GOVERNMENT RECORDS

ibliography

Bureau of Indian Affairs. Records. Annuity Payrolls for the Mdewakanton, Sisseton, and Wahpeton Sioux Tribes, 1853. Record Group 75. National Archives. Washington, D.C.

Commissioner of Indian Affairs, *Annual Report*, 1857.

Commissioner of Indian Affairs, *Annual Report*, 1858.

Documents Relating to the Negotiation of Ratified and Unratified Treaties with Various Tribes of Indians. Record Group 75. National Archives. Washington, D.C.

Fort Ridgely. Letterbook. Letters Received and Sent. Record Group 393. National Archives. Washington, D.C.

Minnesota Superintendency. Letters Received and Sent. Record Group 75. National Archives. Washington, D.C.

Office of Indian Affairs. Letters Received and Sent. Record Group 75. National Archives. Washington, D.C.

———. St. Peter Agency. *Annual Report*, 1855.

St. Peter Agency. Letters Received and Sent. Record Group 75. National Archives. Washington, D.C.

*Statistical Report on the Sickness and Mortality in the Army of the United States.*
3 vols. U.S. Army Surgeon-General's Office. Washington, D.C.:
A.O.P. Nicholson Printers, 1856.

U.S. Congress. *Congressional Serial Set.* Series 550, 919, 920, 1117.

———. *Congressional Serial Set.* House Executive Documents (HED).

U.S. War Department. *The War of the Rebellion: A Compilation of the Official Records of the Union and Confederate Armies.* 128 vols. Washington, D.C.: Government Printing Office, 1891–95.


## MANUSCRIPT COLLECTIONS

*Kansas State Historical Society, Topeka*

William Clark Papers (WCP)

*Minnesota Historical Society, St. Paul*

Theodore G. Carver and Family Papers
William B. Dodd Papers
George W. Doud Diary
Charles Flandrau Papers
Thomas Patrick Gere Journal
Frank Herriot Papers (FHP)
G. Hubert Papers
Martin McLeod Papers
J. A. Nelson Letters
Thomas Scantlebury Diaries
Timothy J. Sheehan Diary
Lawrence Taliaferro Papers, Journal (LTP)
Edward and William Washburn Letters

*South Dakota Historical Society, Pierre*

Doane Robinson Papers


## BOOKS AND ARTICLES

American Battlefield Protection Program. CSWAC Battle Summaries, "Whitestone Hill," http://www.nps.gov/history/hps/abpp/battles/nd004.htm.

American Civil War.com. State Battle Maps, North Dakota, http://www.americancivilwar.com/statepic/nd/nd004.html.

Anonymous. *Fort Ridgely, Minnesota*. Washington, D.C.: War Department, Office of Secretary of War, Adjutant General Fletcher Williams, 1880.

Bakeman, Mary Hawler, comp. and ed. *Legends, Letters, and Lies: Readings on the Spirit Lake Massacre of 1857*. Roseville, Minn.: Park Genealogical Boxes, 2001.

Baker, Miriam Hawthorn. "Inkpaduta's Camp at Smithland." *Annals of Iowa* 39 (Fall 1967): 81–104.

Board of Commissioners, comps. *Minnesota in the Civil War and Indian Wars*. 2 vols. St. Paul: Pioneer Press Company, 1899.

Buck, Daniel. *Indian Outbreaks*. Minneapolis: Ross and Haines, 1965.

Coues, Elliot, ed. *The Expeditions of Zebulon Montgomery Pike*. 2 vols. New York: Francis P. Harper, 1895.

"Crazy Horse's Story of the Custer Fight." *South Dakota Historical Collections*, vol 6. Pierre, S.D.: State Historical Society, 1912.

Daniels, Asa. "Reminiscences of Little Crow." *Collections of the Minnesota Historical Society*. 17 vols. 1908. 12:513–30.

Eastman, Charles. *Indian Boyhood*. New York: McClure and Phillips Co., 1902.

Flandrau, Charles. "The Ink-Pa-Du-Ta Massacre of 1857." *Collections of the Minnesota Historical Society*. 1880. 3:386–407.

Green, Jerome A., ed. *Lakota and Cheyenne: Indian Views of the Great Sioux War, 1876–1877*. Norman: Unviersity of Oklahoma Press, 1994.

Hammer, Kenneth, ed. *Custer in '76: Walter Camp's Notes on the Custer Fight*. Provo, Utah: Brigham Young University, 1976.

Hardorff, Richard G., ed. *Lakota Recollections of the Custer Fight*. Spokane, Wash.: ArthurH. Clark Company, 1991.

Heard, Isaac. *History of the Sioux War and Massacres of 1862 and 1863*. New York: Harper and Brothers Publishers, 1865.

Holcombe, Return I. "Chief Big Eagle's Story of the Sioux Outbreak of 1862." *Collections of the Minnesota Historical Society*. 1894. 6:384–97.

Howe, Orlando C. "The Discovery of the Spirit Lake Massacre." *Annals of Iowa* 11 (July 1914): 409–25.

Keating, William H. *Narrative of an Expedition to the Source of St. Peter's River*. Minneapolis: Ross and Haines, 1959.

"Narrative of Paul Mazakootemane." *Collections of the Minnesota Historical Society*. 1880. 3:82–90.

Oneroad, Amos E., and Alanson B. Skinner. *Being Dakota: Tales and Traditions of the Sisseton and Wahpetons*. Edited by Laura Anderson. St Paul: Minnesota Historical Society Press, 2003.

Pond, Samuel. *The Dakota or Sioux in Minnesota as They Were in 1834.* St. Paul: Minnesota Historical Society Press, 1986.

Randall, B. H. *A Brief Sketch and History of Fort Ridgely.* Fairfax, Minn.: Fairfax Crescent Print, 1896.

Riggs, Stephen R. "Dakota Portraits." *Minnesota History Bulletin* 1 (1915–16): 481–568.

———. *Tah-Koo Wah-Kan; or, The Gospel among the Dakotas.* New York: Arno Press, 1972.

Sharp, Abigail Gardner. *History of the Spirit Lake Massacre.* Des Moines: Wallace-Homestead Book Company, 1971.

Taylor, Joseph Henry. *Twenty Years on the Trap Line.* Bismarck, N.D.: n.p., 1891.

Throne, Mildred, ed. "Iowa Troops in Dakota Territory, 1861–1864." *Iowa Journal of History* 57 (April 1959): 97–193.

Wells, Philip F. "Ninety-six Years among the Indians of the Northwest— Adventures and Reminiscences of an Indian Scout and Interpreter in the Dakotas." *North Dakota Historical Quarterly* 15, no. 2 (April 1948): 85–133.

Williams, William. *The History of Early Fort Dodge and Webster County, Iowa.* Edited by Edward Breen. Fort Dodge, Iowa: KUFD-KFMY, 1950.

Williamson, J. P. Letter to his mother, March 2, 1864. *Minnesota Archaeologist* 20, no. 1 (January 1956): 5–6.

INTERVIEWS BY AUTHOR

Ladonna Brave Bull Allard. April 24, 2007.
Ambrose Little Ghost. May 2, 2007.
Danny Seaboy. May 29, 2007.
Leonard Wabasha. May 29, 2007.

NEWPAPERS

*Chicago Democratic Press*
*Brownsville Southern Minnesota Herald*
*Des Moines Citizen*
*Fairbault Herald*
*Henderson Democrat*
*Mankato Semi-Weekly Record*
*Minnesota Pioneer and Democrat*
*New York Daily Tribune*

*Oskaloosa Herald*
*Pipestone County Star*
*St. Anthony Express*
*St. Cloud Democrat*
*St. Paul Advertiser*
*St. Paul Daily Pioneer and Democrat*
*St. Paul Daily Times*
*St. Paul Pioneer Press*
*St. Paul Daily Press*
*St. Paul Daily Times*
*St. Peter Courier*
*St. Peter Minnesota Free Press*
*Sioux City Eagle*
*Winona Republican*
*Yankton Press and Dakotan*
*Yankton Weekly Dakotan*


## SECONDARY SOURCES

### BOOKS AND ARTICLES

Albright, Samuel J. "The First Organized Government of Dakota." *Collections of the Minnesota Historical Society*. 1898. 8:129–47.

Allison, E. H. "Sioux Proper Names." In *South Dakota Historical Collections*. Pierre: South Dakota State Historical Society, 1912. 6:277.

Anderson, Gary Clayton. *Kinsmen of Another Kind: Dakota–White Relations in the Upper Mississippi Valley, 1650–1862*. Lincoln: University of Nebraska Press, 1984.

———. *Little Crow*. St. Paul: Minnesota Historical Society Press, 1986.

Anderson, Gary Clayton, and Alan R. Woolworth, eds. *Through Dakota Eyes: Narrative Accounts of the Minnesota Indian War of 1862*. St. Paul: Minnesota Historical Society Press, 1986.

Barton, Winifred W. *John P. Williamson: A Brother to the Sioux*. New York: Revell, 1919. Reprint, Clements, Minn.: Sunnycrest Publishing, 1980.

Beck, Paul N. *The First Sioux War: The Grattan Fight and Blue Water Creek, 1854–1856*. Lanham, Md.: University Press of America, 2004.

Blank, Vernon. "Inkpaduatah's Great White Friend." *Iowa Magazine* (December–January 1960–61), 17–19, 48.

Blegen, Theodore C. *Minnesota: A History of the State.* St. Paul: University of Minnesota Press, 1963.

Bonvillain, Nancy. *The Sac and Fox.* New York: Chelsia House Publishers, 1995.

Bristow, David L. "Inkpaduta's Revenge: The True Story of the Spirit Lake Massacre." *The Iowan* (January–February 1999). http://members.aol.com/dlbristow/inkpadut.htm.

Brown, Bob. "The Spirit Lake Massacre." Reprint of six articles from the *Fort Dodge Messenger*, February 18–23, 1957.

Call, Ambrose. "Indians Repelled in Kossuth." *Annals of Iowa* 31, no. 2 (October 1951): 83.

Carley, Kenneth. *The Sioux Uprising of 1862.* St. Paul: Minnesota Historical Society Press, 1961.

Clark, D. E. "The Spirit Lake Massacre." In *Iowa and War*, no. 11, ed. Benjamin F. Shambaugh. Iowa City: State Historical Society of Iowa, 1917–19.

Clodfelter, Michael. *The Dakota War: The United States Army versus the Sioux, 1862–1865.* Jefferson, N.C.: McFarland and Company, 1998.

Coward, John. *The Newspaper Indian: Native American Identity in the Press, 1820–90.* Urbana: University of Illinois Press, 1999.

Diedrich, Mark. *Famous Chiefs of the Eastern Sioux.* Minneapolis: Coyote Books, 1987.

Feraca, Stephen E., and James H. Howard. "The Identity and Demography of the Dakota or Sioux Tribe." *Plains Anthropologist* (May 8–20, 1963): no pp.

Fode, Mark. "Inkpaduta's Bloody Path in 1856 Went through Quarries." *Pipestone County Star*, April 10, 1997. http://www.pipestoneminnesota.com/museum/inky.htm.

Folwell, William Watts. *A History of Minnesota.* 2 vols. St. Paul: Minnesota Historical Society Press, 1961.

Gibbon, Guy. *The Sioux: The Dakota and Lakota Nations.* Oxford: Blackwell Publishing, 2003.

Gilman, Rhoda R. *Henry Hastings Sibley: Divided Heart.* St. Paul: Minnesota Historical Society Press, 2004.

Gray, John S. *Centennial Campaign: The Sioux War of 1876.* Fort Collins, Colo.: Old Army Press, 1976.

Gue, Benjamin. *History of Iowa.* 4 vols. New York: Century History Company, 1903.

Harnack, Curtis. "Prelude to Massacre." *Iowan* 4 (February–March 1956): 36–39.

Herriot, Frank. "Aftermath of the Spirit Lake Massacre." *Annals of Iowa* 18 (1932): 434–70, 482–517, 597–631.

——. "Dr. Isaac H. Harriott." *Annals of Iowa* 18 (1932): 243–94.

——. "The Origins of the Indian Massacre between the Okobojis." *Annals of Iowa* 18 (1932): 323–82.

Hoover, Herbert T. *The Yankton Sioux*. New York: Chelsea House Publications, 1988.

Howard, James H. *The Canadian Sioux*. Lincoln: University of Nebraska Press, 1984.

Hubbard, Lucius and Return Holcombe. *Minnesota in Three Centuries, 1655–1908*. Mankato: Publishing Society of Minnesota, 1908.

Hughes, Thomas. "Causes and Results of the Inkpaduta Massacre." *Collections of the Minnesota Historical Society*. 1912. 14:263–82.

——. *History of Blue Earth County*. Chicago: Middle West Publishing Company, 1909.

——. *Indian Chiefs of Southern Minnesota*. Minneapolis: Ross and Haines, 1969.

——. "The Treaty of Traverse des Sioux in 1851." *Collections of the Minnesota Historical Society*. 1900–1904. 10(1):101–29.

Ingham, Harvey. "Ink-Pa-Du-Tah's Revenge." *Midland Monthly* 4 (July–December 1895): 269–72.

——. "Sioux Indians Harassed the Early Iowa Settlers." *Annals of Iowa* 34 (1957): 137–41.

Jacobson, Clair. "The Battle of Whitestone Hill." *North Dakota History* 44 (Spring 1977): 4–14.

——. "A History of the Yanktonai and Hunkpatina Sioux." *North Dakota History* 47, no. 1 (Winter 1980): 4–24.

Johnson, Fred. *A Glimpse of New Ulm*. New Ulm, Minn.: New Ulm Review Print, 1894.

Jones, Evan. *The Minnesota: Forgotten River*. New York: Holt, Rinehart and Winston, 1962.

Keenan, Jerry. *The Great Sioux Uprising: Rebellion on the Plains, August–September 1862*. Cambridge, Mass.: Da Capo Press, 2003.

Kinsbury, George W. *History of Dakota Territory*. 4 vols. Chicago: S. J. Clarke Publishing Company, 1915.

Landes, Ruth. "Dakota Warfare." *Southwestern Journal of Anthropology* 15 (1959): 43–52.

Landes, Ruth. *The Mystic Lake Sioux: Sociology of the Mdewakantonwan Santee*. Madison: University of Wisconsin Press, 1968.

Larson, Peggy. "Inkpaduta, Renegade Sioux." Master's thesis, Mankato

State University, December 1969, available at Iowa State Historical
  Library.
———. "A New Look at the Elusive Inkpaduta." *Minnesota History* 48, no.
  1 (Spring 1982): 24–35.
Laut, Agnes C. "Pioneer Women of the West: The Heroines of Spirit
  Lake, Iowa." *The Outing* 51 (March 1908): 686–698.
Lee, L. P. *History of the Spirit Lake Massacre*. Iowa City: State Historical
  Society of Iowa, 1918.
Meyer, Roy. "The Canadian Sioux: Refugees from Minnesota." *Minnesota History* 41 (Spring 1968): 13–28.
Meyer, Roy. *History of the Santee Sioux*. Lincoln: University of Nebraska
  Press, 1984.
Miller, David Humphreys. *Custer's Fall: The Native American Side of the
  Story*. New York: Meridan Press, 1992.
Morris, Lucy Leavenworth Wilder, ed. *Old Rail Fence Corners: Frontier
  Tales Told by Minnesota Pioneers*. St. Paul: Minnesota Historical Society
  Press, 1976.
Paulson, Howard. "Federal Indian Policy and the Dakota Indians."
  *South Dakota History* 3, no. 3 (Summer 1973): 285–309.
Petersen, William. "The Spirit Lake Massacre." *Palimpsest* 38 (June
  1957): 209–72.
Peterson, Harold. "Wahkonsa." *Palimpsest* 23, no. 4 (April 1942): 121–35.
Potter, Theodore E. "Recollections of Minnesota Experiences." *Minnesota History Bulletin* 2 (1917–18): 419–521.
Pratt, H. M. *History of Fort Dodge and Webster County, Iowa*. Chicago:
  Pioneer Publishing Company, 1913.
Robinson, Doane. *A History of the Dakota or Sioux Indians*. Minneapolis:
  Ross and Haines, 1956.
Roddis, Louis H. *The Indian Wars of Minnesota*. Cedar Rapids, Iowa:
  Torch Press, 1956.
Rose, Arthur P. *An Illustrated History of Jackson County, Minnesota*. Jackson, Minn.: Northern History Publishing Company, 1910.
Rosenberg, Morton M. "The People of Iowa on the Eve of the Civil
  War." *Annals of Iowa* 39 (Fall 1967): 105–33.
Schell, Herbert S. *History of South Dakota*. Lincoln: University of Nebraska Press, 1975.
Schultz, Duane. *Over the Earth I Come: The Great Sioux Uprising of 1862*.
  New York: St. Martin's Press, 1992.
Sibley, H. H. "Sketch of John Other Day." *Collections of the Minnesota
  Historical Society*. 1880. 3:99–102.

Smith, R. A. *A History of Dickerson County, Iowa*. Des Moines: Kenyon Printing and Mfg. Company, 1902.

Stewart, Edgar I. *Custer's Luck*. Norman: University of Oklahoma Press, 1955.

Taylor, Joseph Henry. "Inkpaduta and Sons." *North Dakota Historical Quarterly* 4, no. 3. (October 1929–July 1930): 153–64.

Teakle, Thomas. *The Spirit Lake Massacre*. Iowa City: State Historical Society of Iowa, 1918.

Turning Bear. "Inkpaduta Santee, 1815–1882." In *Fort Peck Assiniboine and Sioux History* (1900), http://www.montana.edu/wwwfpcc/tribes/santee.html.

Utley, Robert M. *Frontiersmen in Blue: The United States Army and the Indian, 1848–1865*. Lincoln: University of Nebraska Press, 1981.

———. *The Lance and The Shield: The Life and Times of Sitting Bull*. New York: Henry Holt Company, 1993.

Van Nuys, Maxwell. *Inkpaduta — the Scarlet Point: Terror of the Dakota Frontier and Secret Hero of the Sioux*. N.p.: privately published, 1998.

Wall, Joseph Frazier. *Iowa: A Bicentennial History*. New York: W. W. Norton, 1978.

Welch, James, and Paul Stekler. *Killing Custer: The Battle of the Little Big Horn and the Fate of the Plains Indians*. New York: W. W. Norton, 1994.

White, Richard. "The Winning of the West: The Expansion of the Western Sioux in the Eighteenth Century." In *Major Problems in American Indian History*, ed. Albert Hurtado and Peter Iverson, 243–57. Lexington, Mass.: D.C. Heath and Company, 1994.

Woolworth, Alan, and Nancy Woolworth. "Eastern Dakota Settlement and Subsistence Patterns Prior to 1851." *Minnesota Archaeologist* 39, no. 2 (May 1980): 70–89.

Wozniak, John S. *Contact, Negotiation, and Conflict: An Ethnohistory of the Eastern Dakota, 1819–1839*. Washington, D.C.: University Press of America, 1978.

# Index